Words for Images *A Gallery of Poems*

Words for Images *A Gallery of Poems*

Edited by John Hollander and Joanna Weber

Yale University Art Gallery, New Haven, Connecticut

This publication is made possible by the kind patronage
of Lindsay P. McCrum (1980), Nina and Lee Griggs (1951),
the Mr. and Mrs. George R. Rowland, B.A. 1933, Fund, and the
Katharine Ordway Fund and was organized in conjunction
with Yale University's Tercentennial celebrations and National
Poetry Month, April 2001.

An accompanying exhibition entitled *A Gallery of Poems*
is scheduled for August 21–November 4, 2001, at the Yale
University Art Gallery.

Frontispiece: 1999 reinstallation of the permanent galleries
of European and Contemporary Art, third floor Louis Kahn
building. Photo credit: Carl Kaufman.

Library of Congress Cataloging-in-Publication Data
Words for images : a gallery of poems / edited by John
Hollander and Joanna Weber.
     p. cm.
   ISBN 0-89467-096-4 (alk. paper)
     1. Art—Poetry. 2. American poetry—20th century. 3. Yale
University. Art Gallery—Poetry.   I. Hollander, John. II. Weber,
Joanna, 1959-   .
  PS595.A75 W67 2001
  811´.54080357—dc21

                              2001024081

1701 2001

Contents

Director's Foreword

Words for Images: A Gallery of Poems comprises a direct literary response to selected twentieth-century artworks residing in the Yale Art Gallery's collections, presenting new writing commissioned from twenty-two Yale-trained poets. John Hollander, Sterling Professor of English, and Joanna Weber, the Gallery's Assistant Curator of European and Contemporary Art, are to be thanked for conceiving this creative project in celebration of Yale community's Tercentennial. They have brought it to life with the full support of the Gallery's staff and the kind patronage of Lindsay P. McCrum (1980), Nina and Lee Griggs (1951), the Mr. and Mrs. George R. Rowland, B.A. 1933, Fund, and the Katharine Ordway Fund.

Each poet whom Hollander and Weber invited to participate in this project was free to choose the specific artwork that piqued his or her interest and imagination. The writers' visual discoveries thus directly inspired the creation of the new poems you are about to read. The poets were also afforded complete freedom to craft the form and content of their work as they pleased.

Many of the artworks selected for literary treatment have been donated to Yale by some of its most distinguished alumni collectors, dedicated patrons such as Bruce Dayton, B.A. 1940, Charles Seymour, Jr., B.A. 1935, Richard Brown Baker, B.A. 1935, and Stephen Carlton Clark, B.A. 1903. Other works chosen by the poets arrived as defining gifts to the Gallery from individuals who deeply valued this teaching museum's central mission and wished to nurture a fuller understanding of twentieth-century art among students and scholars. The Société Anonyme collection, for example, assembled by collector Katherine Dreier and artist Marcel Duchamp, now forms the central spine of Yale's European and American modern art collection and is well represented in this volume with poems written in response to artworks created by Kasimir Malevich, Sophie Taeuber-Arp, Kurt Schwitters, Marcel Duchamp, and Joseph Stella. So too is the renowned Katharine Ordway Collection, providing works by Pierre Bonnard and Mark Rothko to the attention of our writers. It may be less obvious that some of the artists whose work is included in this volume matriculated at Yale. Mark Rothko studied at the University for two years as an undergraduate (1921–23), Claes Oldenburg attended Yale from 1946–50, and Sylvia Plimack Mangold graduated from the Yale School of Art in 1961. Others will surely remember Walker Evans's (1903–75) tenure as professor of graphic design at the Yale School of Art, and how his remarkable artistic vision helped shape Yale's photography program to this day. Tod Papageorge currently holds the endowed Walker Evans Professorship at the Yale School of Art, where a new generation of artists is being trained by a distinguished faculty of practicing artists. At

Yale, therefore, a new generation of artists continues to be trained by a distinguished faculty of practicing artists.

Yale, as this volume will demonstrate, has also played an important role in encouraging many of its students to dedicate their talents and lives to the field of creative writing. Numerous graduates are now sustaining professional careers in the field of contemporary literature, some of which have earlier been recognized and honored by the University's annual Younger Poets Awards program. We happily celebrate the achievements of all the artists associated with this project as the Yale Art Gallery enters a new century of service to the University and world culture.

Jock Reynolds
The Henry J. Heinz II, Director
Yale University Art Gallery

Preface & Acknowledgments

A thinker is very much like a draughtsman whose aim
it is to represent all the interrelations between things.
Ludwig Wittgenstein, *Culture and Value*

Poets and artists are thinkers. Their work expands our ability to link ideas in new and unusual combinations. Our participation through reading, listening, looking—gives depth to our everyday experience of things and transforms the ordinary.

The essential goal behind *Words for Images* was to encourage poets to interact with art objects. There is a long tradition of the reciprocal relationship between poets and artists which John Hollander discusses in his introduction. However, in this book we bring poets who were once students back to the Yale campus. The interaction between word and object located at the Art Gallery celebrates the art of poetry and the museum's collection and reflects the direct contemplative contact between poet and object.

The project emerged from a dinner conversation I had with John Hollander, when we plotted commissioning Yale poets on twentieth-century works of art at the Yale University Art Gallery on the occasion of Yale's Tercentennial. As editors, we made the final selections, based on the poets' choices with a concern for balance, not only of medium but nationality and chronology for the publication and the exhibition.

The book's layout juxtaposes twenty-two poems and images followed by paired commentaries by us on the particular object and poem and is organized chronologically based on the works of art.

This has been a wonderful project. Special thanks must go to the poets themselves. In the Department of European and Contemporary Art, Jennifer Gross, the Seymour H. Knox, Jr., Curator was always available to review, yet again, our drafts. Yvonne Morant cheerfully shepherded the project forward. Graduate students Emily Breault, Clay Dean, and Susan Greenberg, and undergraduate Mariana Mogilevich enthusiastically supported this work. Carl Kaufman handled all the new photography. Sonia Shannon, the award-winning graphic designer for Craig Arnold's book of poetry, *Shells* (1999), put this book together. Judy Zimmer of Thames Printing handled the production while Joyce Ippolito carefully edited it.

Without institutional support, no project can move forward as smoothly as has this one. To Jock Reynolds, director of the Yale Art Gallery, we are indebted. Finally, this book would never have been possible without John Hollander. His soft-spoken manner and his hard work determined its success. To him I am particularly grateful.

Emily Dickinson once observed that

There is no frigate like a book
To take us lands away
Nor any Courses like a page

To Emily Dickinson's homage to poetry, as a curator I might add that there is also nothing like an image to move and redirect one's life. In this book, we have both: poetry and works of art, words for images, and now the Yale University Art Gallery has its own Gallery of Poems.

Joanna Weber
Assistant Curator
Department of European and Contemporary Art
Yale University Art Gallery

Introduction

Poetry directed to particular works—today generally called "ecphrastic" —of art goes back to some of our earliest literature. It has its origins in a slightly different sort of poetry, describing a purely fictional graphic or sculpted image which only comes into being in the lines of the poem. Celebrated examples of this kind of "notional ecphrasis" (of an imagined image) are that of the shield of Achilles in Homer's *Iliad*, and of that of Herakles by Hesiod, the description of carved images on a cup in the first Idyll of Theocritus, Virgil's telling of Aeneas's encounter with painted scenes of the Trojan war in a temple in Carthage, and later on in the *Aeneid* an ecphrasis of the hero's armor and shield, Ovid's description of the images Arachne and Athena were weaving in their fabric, and following this, Dante's relief carvings in Canto X of the *Purgatorio*. These were all notional ecphrasis, inventing the works of art they were describing. But there were also short epigrammatic poems from the Greek Anthology that literally addressed actual works of art. In one instance well known in the Renaissance, a poem by Posidippus puts a statue by the poet's contemporary Lysippus (ca. 270 B.C.E.) of *Kairos* (opportunity) through an interrogation about its appearance and attributes, and working the statue's answers, giving the correct allegorical interpretations, into its lines.

Then in Renaissance epic, the long narrative poems of Ariosto, Tasso, Spenser, and Shakespeare in *The Rape of Lucrece* all have one or more episodes when a painting or tapestry is described; in a subsequent tradition romantic lyric, rather than narrative poems, begins to deal with the personal experience of seeing a particular work of art, and this tradition has continued through modernist poetry to the present day. A common Renaissance theme was that of the *paragone,* or contention for primacy among the arts, and any poem about a picture or piece of sculpture might be thought of as touching at that matter, even if only implicitly. Also, a moralizing or emblematic impulse remains always present; and in modern poetry there is a developing sense of language's inadequacy to comprehend image, although it is only language's vast capacities which allow it to consider its own limits. There seems to be a degree to which poem and painting or sculpture are almost erotically related, language always seeking to embrace image, its desire always thwarted, so that the poem is like a Petrarchan lover and the painting the mistress whose very gaze chastens and sublimates.

Then, too, poems always in some sense construct the works of art they purport to see: the power of their gaze to focus on all sorts of elements—even invisible ones which seem, in the poem's gaze, to rise to the surface—comes at the price of *not* noticing so much else. There is a degree to which all poetic addresses to, or considerations of, particular

Peter Paul Rubens (Flemish, 1577–1640), *Hero and Leander*, ca. 1605. oil on canvas, 56 x 128 cm. Gift of Susan Morse Hilles. 1962.25

works of art—what has been called "actual ecphrasis"—partakes of the "notional ecphrasis," or description of a purely imaginary work of art, mentioned at the beginning. For if the artist can claim "I paint what I see," the poem will always see the painting as the artist sees the world that he or she has painted, saying "I see what I say." And to this degree, the poem is always describing or addressing or speaking for, or out of, a notional work of art of its own.

Several paintings and prints in the Yale University Art Gallery have received this kind of poetic treatment in the past. The most celebrated of these is perhaps Peter Paul Rubens's *Hero and Leander* (1605), illustrating a moment in the famous story of the drowning of the young Leander in the Hellespont, across which he swims every night from Abydos to Sestos to meet with his lover, Hero.[1] After hearing of his death in the waves, Hero plunges into them as well and drowns herself. The Italian baroque poet Giambattista Marino (1569–1625) had probably seen the painting in Mantua before 1610: five years after that, Marino had completed his fascinating *La Galeria*, a collection of more than six hundred poems about works of art, both imaginary and actual. His poem on the Rubens painting is one of the few for which the actual work is precisely identifiable and survives to this day. Marino treats the scene in a manner typical of earlier ecphrastic poetry, which addresses persons or objects in

1. The poetic responses to this work are discussed in detail in Amy Golahny, "Rubens' *Hero and Leander*," *Yale Art Gallery Bulletin,* 1990, 20–37.

the painting, often with regard to some narrative in the picture. (In more modern poems it is more as if to ascribe some kind of responsibility to the work of art for implying some latent or hidden story or agenda.) In the Rubens painting, the arms of the nymphs form, for Marino, a kind of living coffin (what Milton called "a watery bier") and the poet looks ahead to the further consequences—not depicted here—of Hero's seeing the drowned body of her beloved, thus resulting in what he calls the *maggior crudeltà* ("greater cruelty") of Hero's suicide:

> Where, O you sea-nymphs, where
> With such a pitiless pity do you bear
> The funeral hearse of the wretch
> Of Abydos, he whose burning
> Of love and vital light were quenched in the churning
> Spume of your cruel barbaric element?
> No—why at Sestos do you
> Display him on the shore, bloodless and spent?
> A greater cruelty than killing him.
> Is thus to place him in his lady's view.

> [tr. John Hollander]

Later, in the 1650s, the famous Dutch poet Joost von den Vondel adapted Marion's poem to a sonnet of his own, followed by Jan Vos in another much longer (forty-odd line) poem. Rubens's painting, whose subject matter itself derived from poems by Ovid and the much later Musaeus, might be said to mediate between two bodies of poetry, illustrating one, interpreted by the other.

The early-nineteenth-century New York poet Joseph Rodman Drake wrote an extremely amusing set of verses on John Trumbull's *The Declaration of Independence* (completed 1786), a huge replica of which he had seen on exhibition in New York. The first two stanzas give an idea of the tone throughout:

John Trumbull
(American, 1756–1843)

The Declaration of Independence, 4 July 1776, 1786–1820
Oil on canvas
53.7 x 79.1 cm
Trumbull Collection
1832.3

The National Painting

Awake, ye forms of verse divine!
  Painting! descend on canvas wing,—
And hover o'er my head, Design!
  Your son, your glorious son, I sing:
At Trumbull's name I break my sloth,
  To load him with poetic riches:
The Titian of a table-cloth!
  The Guido of a pair of breeches!

Come, star-eyed maid, Equality!
  In thine adorer's praise I revel;
Who brings, so fierce his love to thee,
  All forms and faces to a level:
Old, young, great, small, the grave, the gay,
  Each man might swear the next his brother,
And there they stand in dread array,
  To fire their votes at one another.

Drake here pokes fun at the documentary character of Trumbull's painting, which seeks to include all the original signers of the celebrated document. He mocks as well what he feels to be the excessively anti-heroic quality of such a benign visual event manifesting a crucial one in the foundation of a democratic republic.

One more example might be given—again, of a very different sort—of a poem directed to a painting in the Yale Art Gallery. J. D. McClatchy, a contemporary poet (and editor of *The Yale Review*; he has also contributed a poem to this volume) approaches Giovanni Paolo Panini's *Capriccio of Roman Ruins and Sculpture with Figures* of 1741 with an informed eye as well as a speculating gaze. The painting rearranges structures in the Forum, in some instances (the Arch of Titus, the Farnesian gardens, the Palatine maintain their actual positions in relation to each other), but most of the monuments in the scene have been moved about, with the effect of creating a sort of stage set for the figures the painter introduces. McClatchy starts out his longish (62-line) meditation with straightforward but extremely selective and consciously tendentious description of the scene, a basic device of many modern ecphrastic poems:

The light starts in a promising street,
Edges the stolen slabs of another art,
Up pitted columns, pediment by leaf,
And casts their shadows against the graying
Academy of clouds suspended above
An imagined forum as if in disbelief—
Airy element we too are in, until
Trappings catch they eye as they will...

A nude giant the world holds up,
Porphyry putti adoring death's home
Away from harm. The motto on these ruins
Reads *Restore.*[2]

Giovanni Paolo Panini
(Italian, Rome,
1691–1764/86)

*A Capriccio of Roman
Ruins and Sculpture
with Figures*, 1741
Oil on canvas
174 x 219.7 cm
Stephen Carlton Clark,
B.A. 1903, Fund
1964.41

Each of the poems collected here was written, specifically for this
volume, by a poet with a degree from Yale, in connection with a particular
object of twentieth-century art in the Yale Art Gallery. The extremely
loose term "in connection with" reflects the wide variety of possible
stances, mentioned previously, which a poem can take toward a work of
art, and therefore variously *on* it, *about* it, *to* it, speaking out *as* it or as
something *in* it, answering some question the work of art itself never, of
course, audibly asked, and so many others. Just as a range of objects—
painting, print, sculpture, photograph, object of industrial design—is
addressed in these texts, the poems themselves exhibit a very wide range
of formal modes and rhetorical stances. They also display an even wider
range of ways of dealing with the object in question.

For one thing, many poets of the later twentieth century have had
considerable exposure to art-historical teaching and writing: they notice
things—albeit as poets—that scholarship has taught them to see almost as
inhering in the work of art itself. For another, they have behind (or would
it be better to say, "within") them a considerable history of ecphrastic
poetry, from Homer until the present day. The effect of this is to produce
in each case some agenda of revision, almost always unacknowledged in
the poem, of some mode of poem in that tradition. The reader will notice,
among the poems and visual objects paired here, not only a variety of

2. "A Capriccio of Roman Ruins with Sculpture and Figures," from *Scenes from Another Life.*
Copyright © 1981 by J. D. McClatchy. Reprinted by permission. Other works in the Art Gallery's
collection have been handled by poets such as James Thomson ("B.V."), on Albrecht Dürer's
Melencolia I; Randall Jarrell on Dürer's *The Knight, Death and the Devil*; Irving Feldman on one of
Goya's *Disasters of War*; and John Hollander on Thomas Eakins, *William Rush and His Model.* For
a discussion of these, and of ecphrastic poetry generally, see Hollander's *The Gazer's Spirit* (1995).

stances toward the visual object, but toward various ideas of what a poem *to* or *about* a work might be. It is instructive to consider in which cases the poet has given his or her poem the same title as that of the work of art, or an entirely different one. Furthermore, the remarkable diversity of formal modes that characterizes the best American poetry of the last part of the twentieth century will also be apparent in these texts, as well as a variety of ways in which the verse form and structure may or may not represent something in what the poet "sees" in the work of art, or something in his or her particular mode of poetic talking in a particular poem. The poems vary from those in rhymed accentual-syllabic verse to three very different instances in which the poet has himself produced a piece of graphic art, of the typographical sort—in one case, as one of his two responses to the painting.

John Hollander
Sterling Professor of English
Yale University

Words for Images *A Gallery of Poems*

Stephen Cushman
The Ploughmen

lean so hard in their harness they practically lie down
face-first in the field, a piece they haven't furrowed yet,

each nearly parallel to flat horizon and band
of blank sky in the distance and overhead that dark

sheet of cloud, bounding some front that could be sliding in
from behind us, as the two men lean from right to left

against the grain of reading. What happened to the ox or
ass or horse that should be pulling the plow instead

of them? And who are they anyhow? Father and son,
the former no more than a background shadow, his head

dropped toward the dirt, as though refusing to see how far
they have to go before they reach the end of the row

and need to turn the plow around? The moment of slack
in the harness straps feels sweet on the shoulders. But then

it all begins again, the heave against inertia,
the cursing and guttural groans as worn straps tighten

into lashed skin and another whole row lies ahead
with nothing to ease its length except perhaps a word

from the possible son, his mouth open just enough
to shape the sounds of exertion, the beastly straining,

into *weiter, Väterchen*; yet even if he's not
the son, he's plainly the source of light in the etching,

white shirt and brow assigned the work of holding at bay
the black in that landscape. Clearly Käthe loved the line

of his back, modeling, maybe, his face on her own
boy Peter, who died in war and took the light with him.

The primary subject matter of Käthe Kollwitz's oeuvre was the struggle of daily life. She was influenced by Emile Zola's social realism—she illustrated an edition of his novel *Germinal*—and was an established artist in the Berlin circle. Working primarily on paper, she presented human suffering in a sympathetic manner. This particular etching of agricultural production shows two individuals pulling the plough, their beasts of burden clearly dead. The work of these ploughmen is presented with dignity. Commitment and struggle to provide sustenance for loved ones gives this etching force. JW

In a device of modernist poetry pioneered by Marianne Moore and William Carlos Williams, Cushman's title here immediately turns out to be the opening of his first line, thus calling attention to the fact that his poem's title is a bit referentially ambiguous: *The Ploughmen* is Käthe Kollwitz's print, but "the ploughmen" of the title first line are the straining figures represented in it. The poem immediately focuses on them both narratively— "a piece they haven't plowed yet"—and, in a more modern sense, pictorially—"each nearly parallel to flat horizon and band / of blank sky" (and, at the end, a similar characterization of "white shirt and brow assigned the work of holding at bay / the black in that landscape"). But in general, the poem's strategy is more directly to tell the story that the print keeps to itself, even writing a verbal utterance ("*weiter, Vaterchen*"— "further on, Daddy") for the son it has taken the more prominent figure to be. And yet it is in the poem's own interpretive uncertainty ("yet even if he's not the son") that leads to the invocation of the artist's own absent son at the powerful and far from sentimental conclusion.

Cushman's poem is formed of thirteen unrhyming couplets of lines of thirteen syllables, but there is nothing numerologically symbolic about this, save perhaps that the form may stand in a revisionary way for the sonnet form used by so much ecphrastic poetry from the Renaissance on—almost as if the rectangular format of a sonnet set in type mirrored in some way a rectangular framed picture. JH

The Principle of Flickering
John Burt

Ever more, human culture is being made of iron, ever more machine-like,
ever more resembling a vast laboratory where revenge on the forces of
nature is preparing: science grows in order to subjugate the earth; art
grows, a winged dream, a mysterious aeroplane for escape from the earth;
industry grows so that people can leave the earth behind them.—Alexander
Blok

I

At nine he stood all night to watch the storm,
The furious sky, the boiling clouds aswirl,
No longer clouds or sky but jagged blazes
Splintered and scattered as if space fell in
And things burned through to stark ideas of things
And then to figure, number, and the dark.

His father said: "Machines will do the work,
Will slice the beets and soak the sugar out,
And bleach the crystals in the centrifuge."

His Grinder is as sharp as what he grinds,
And as metallic—the man, more than his wheel,
Is a machine, a brittle stack of shards
And cones and polygons popped halfway out
From stairs and banisters and paving blocks
All made of his same stuff (all made of thought).

II

It's still things as they are he grinds and grinds,
Not as they might have been, no blazoned man
Perfected into steel, beyond the mess
Of inconvenient lymph and sperm and tears
And squishy nonmetallic friends and kin,
The sentimental flight from sentiment,
Whose beauty is just force, whose love is death
In glorious but nonexistent Rome
(That was the past's future, *a never was*
That never got to *couldn't be* or *won't,*
Not man perfected but no longer man,
A hard dry almost lifelike marionetti,

A faceted whirling autopilot drone),
No plane or factory or dynamo
To bend each mind along its lines of force,
But just a craftsman, electric in his craft,
His arm in motion here, and here, across
His turning body, pressing with both hands
The bucking knife against the storm of stone,
His working foot, his knee now tense, now flexed
Here, then here, his left hand arcing over,
His turning head straight on, hunched, peering down
Past antique, bristling, crank moustachios
And then in profile: nose, pursed lips, whiskers,
Another chin sketched in, this time in brown—
Still peasant even in that harlequin,
As much in Repin's world as in Picasso's.

III
But what's his wont, his project for the sun?
To be not man, nor yet machine, but motion,
Flesh gulping after form, then formlessness,
A cyclone of little planes sprayed out like grit,
An edge propped firm to grind another edge,
To grind all things to patterns, stuff to shapes,
Words to sound, thoughts to *zaum*, to wake
A truth beyond all objects: Plato's chaos
In Heraclitus' cave, the virtual cones
Swept out by zigging lines:
                              "I wished to free
The painted shapes from shapes of things, from earth.
Nothing stays fastened down, jailed in mass.
I've broken the horizon's stapled ring,
I've ripped the blue lampshade, swum into white
Not just to copy objects but to know.
Swim out, oh aeronauts, swim after me."
Victory over stone and knife and sun.
Victory over his brown moustachios.

IV
"Arise, ye prisoners of the flesh, the dirt:
Here's a new dress, a brand new kind of teapot,
A motor with no steam or gasoline.
Come smiths, come braziers, concrete pavers come,
Come foundrymen and tailors, fitters and miners,
Come clothe the world afresh in bare delight."

They didn't get it. They knew he meant them well,
For all his hard cold system spun from thought.
They liked the posters, made nothing of *planit*
And *architecton*, buildings for the moon.
It was his freedom, his hunger for the real,
The absolutely real, disguised as halls
And factories and workers' public baths.
"Your problem, Ilyich, is: you just want things."
"Yours, Kazimir: you want all time and space."

Well, things won out—Stakhanov, the big broad dams,
The worker, the farmer (the worker kerchiefed, female),
The intellectual (the same old worker
This time in spectacles, hefting a book),
Mystic figures literally made concrete
As Gorky wanted: Show what must be done
Then show just how to do it, plan by plan.
That's *Realism*. That too was an idea,
A self-disowned idea, a brutal trance
Driven by a specter, not the real.
He was exhibit A of Bourgeois Art,
The gaudy jetsam of decaying states,
Went back to painting figures, saved his skin,
But was buried with an avantgardist stone.

The grave, near Leningrad, was lost to war.
No one knows exactly where it is.
Somewhere, in a *planit* in the Real
Our Kazimir is on the porch with Proust
And Lobachevsky, laughing over tea.

Kasimir Malevich
(Russian, 1878–1935)

The Knifegrinder, 1912–13
Oil on canvas
79.5 x 79.5 cm
Gift of the Société Anonyme
1941.553

Known primarily for pioneering the shift to abstraction, Kasimir Malevich's oeuvre as a whole is indicative of the various directions arising from the fracturing of the figure plane, first explored by Pablo Picasso and Georges Braque with Cubism. This painting is an example of Malevich's early representational work and captures a series of moments in the action of sharpening knives. Painted in the Cubo-Futurist tradition, this square painting vibrates, shakes, and makes noise. JW

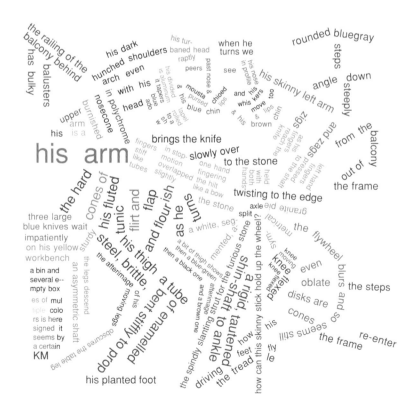

John Burt's blank-verse discourse is directed to the painting in question, but also even more toward the world in which Malevich practiced his art and which he shared with all the other remarkable painters, sculptors, and designers upon whom Stalin was venting his murderous wrath after the 1920s. Modernist and progressive art like Malevich's was designated as reactionary, "formalist," and bourgeois, as opposed to the officially sanctioned "socialist realism." Some of the historical details in these lines should be glossed for today's reader: the Russian word *zaum* in part III means "nonsense" (particularly with regard to incoherence). Ilya Efimovich Repin (1844–1930) was a portraitist and anecdotal painter whom Stalinist cultural repression made into an icon of approved socialist realism; *planit* and *architecton* are Malevich's own names for unbuildable, visionary architectural structures; Aleksey Stakhanov was a coal miner after whom in the mid-1930s an officially sanctioned speed-up system for increased worker output in the Soviet Union was named. Nikolay Ivanovich Lobachevski was a Russian mathematician of the early nineteenth century, one of the founders of non-Euclidean geometry, and Burt brings him together with Malevich and Proust at the very end of the poem in a delightful constellation. The poet is here concerned with the question of how, as Wallace Stevens put it, "Realism is a corruption of reality," and indeed, the "things as they are" he starts out parts II and III with revisionist echoes of lines from Wallace Stevens's *The Man with the Blue Guitar*.

In the course of thinking about it, Burt composed a much less discursive ecphrasis of the painting, a fascinating kind of glossorial sketch. It raises wonderful questions about image and word, abstraction and concreteness, and recursiveness, all the while paying a joyful homage to Futurism and Constructivism. JH

Spring (The Procession)
Rachel Wetzsteon

after Joseph Stella

i.

And had it come to this?
All winter the leaves clung to the branches
and snow, withheld as an angry god's
or an old globe's accusation, never fell.
Fierce disorder followed: sleds languished;
sidewalks smelled of pine and lilac;
coats hung—dusty, comical—on high pegs.
White was a memory. And when spring came
it was only a name, a fact on a page
without the corresponding colors
that blared their message over town, shouting
You struggled through the cold, hard winter
now bloom on cue: be like me, be this green.

ii.

What could the downcast lovers of seasons do
but flee the warm city into springs
of their own making? And soon there were plenty:
false springs that came and went before breakfast;
strange springs that worried the downstairs neighbors;
fugitive springs that bad moods scared away.
But most of all there were lonely springs,
sudden flashes of insight that grandly promised
starlit gazebos and an end to hunger....
But the open window still opened on hunger
and the long street showed no sign of the mind's big day.

iii.

A thousand leaves rush forward:
bright, like an image of something lost,
quick, like a portent of something fast
becoming a page in a tear-stained book
that people look at in separate rooms, thinking
There was a thing called spring, and it gave
my better days a meaning. But now

that it's always spring, the days mean nothing;
the word's been bled of its earthy realness
and as the heat rises, to what in the world
can I ever compare my wildly leaping heart?

iv.

Down the various leaf-strewn paths we go,
she muttered sadly to her oldest friend,
the one she had walked with arm in arm
down all those broad alleys
through so many springs. He nodded, saying
We're on two roads now, heading away
from that marriage of reverie and green
too happy to last. Unless....Unless?
Unless, sitting together in a ruined garden,
lost in distinctly chilly thoughts,
we sense traces of our favorite season
stirring around us, gathering weight and form:
I plan a punch line but you beat me to it;
a vagrant petal grazes first your arm, then mine;
a small bird lands on a stone bench and starts to sing.
When I stare down my narrow alley
a low voice says badness, madness, sadness;
but something happens when we look at the bird
and, looking together, invite it to stay.
A minute ago we were lost as winter
but now we're all headed in the same direction—
you, me, the bird, and this late spring day.

Joseph Stella
(American, born Italy, 1877–1946)

Spring (The Procession), ca. 1914–16
Oil on canvas
191.5 x 102.3 cm
Gift of Collection Société Anonyme
1941.692

This celebration of color is stylistically handled in the tradition of Italian Futuristic tradition. Stella presents a May Day parade in his native Italy by clustering small triangles of color. The Maypoles break the rectangularity of the canvas, and the density of the triangles is modified throughout the surface though this work is not immediately grasped rationally. Stella, referred to as the first American Futurist, appeals to emotion, trapped by memories of the explosion of spring, and to individuals becoming one joyous crowd. JW

Imagination is always working to free the mind from routines of perception and stock responses to what is perceived. In contemplating a joyfully constructed visual song to spring, with its abstracted leaflike forms, gradations among browns and green, ladderlike structures heading up toward a skyey blue, this poem fuels a call to shed itself of the banalities of "springtime," however welcome even they can seem after a bad late winter. And here, too, as in the case of several of the poems in this collection, the painting's title—dissociated from May Day parading—has become part of the object of meditation. Various "processions" arise as types and foreshadowings of the central procession of the seasons themselves: sequences of particular springs of particular years, proceeding down a path of recollection; fallen autumnal leaves that "rush forward" in the wind of time; the slow procession, in the last section, of a pair of longtime friends down an actual garden path. And we are reminded that poems themselves, "downcast lovers of seasons," contrive to "flee... into springs / of their own making." At the end of this one, the reader has herself or himself been led, through the unrhymed four- and five-beat lines, to work through to a recovery, like that of the year itself. In this case, it is a recovery of a quickened immediate sense of spring, innocently free of the pressures of memory and analytic self-consciousness through which it necessarily had, at the outset, to submit itself. JH

rachel wetzsteon 15

Kurt Schwitters's Real Name

Jonathan Aaron

> He believed, with Heraclitus,
> that the sun is only as big as it seems to be
> —Jean Arp (from his elegy for K.S.)

Kurt Hermann Eduard Karl Julius Schwitters:
"I am a painter, I nail my pictures together."
He loved nonsense, he said, because he felt sorry for it.
After the war, since everything had broken down,

the new could only be created from fragments.
Merz—a syllable that bears repeating until
it starts to mean what it says—rescued
by chance one day in 1919

from a newspaper advertisement
for the Kommerz-und Privatbank.
The word declaring itself for the first time
like one of the big electric signs flashing

above the seething streets of Hannover or Berlin.
What's left of commerce without community,
an echo of the Roman god of thieves,
four sevenths of the German word for pain.

Merz, he decided was his own real name,
and the name for everything he'd go on to make
from scraps of trash and refuse.
But in his *Merzzeichnungen*, or Merz-drawings,

his sketches with wastepaper, he couldn't help portraying
a vista. Take *Merzz 19*, this little
stained-glass window hinting
the ghost of whoever leans in

for a closer look at a war tax stamp
from a pack of cigarettes, potato ration stamps,
a streetcar ticket, the number *37*,
remnants of Saturday

and Sunday, wrapping paper bearing the design
of an impossible labyrinth—everything

in the process of lifting like a flock of pigeons,
slowly, then more urgently

into a glimpse of rushing cloud and sky.
Aphorisms for the eye
framed in snatches of an exploded grammar
(what other kind was there?)

about not enough food, a ruined currency, crowds
in lines, uncertain destinations,
the indifference of time. And the pale-blue
cutting of an unused registration form

like a premonition
that he himself would eventually become
to all but a few
someone who never existed.

In a photograph his son took in 1947,
he's alone on a rocky knoll
in England's Lake District,
brightness and overcast,

water, then hills in the distance.
He always believed in landscape.
He never forgot the line of the horizon.
He hated throwing anything away.

Kurt Schwitters
(German, 1887–1948)

Merzz. 19, 1920
Paper collage
31.7 x 23.1 cm
Gift of the Société Anonyme
1941.681
© 2001 Artists Rights Society (ARS), New York / VG Bild-Kunst, Bonn

Merz, the nonsense term Schwitters gave to his collages and assemblages, is an invented Dada name. A member of the early Dada movement in Berlin, he is also well known for his poems, particularly *Anna Blume,* first published in *Der Sturm*, 1919. Mixing Dada concepts with constructions, he builds poems in his collages with found objects—tickets, newspaper—fragments of daily life. *Merzz* departs from traditional art making in both medium and in subject matter, and Schwitters even called himself *Merzz. Merzz. 19* belongs to a group of collages that Schwitters called *Merzzeichnungen—Merzz* drawings. JW

Schwitters was a Dadaist poet as well as an artist, and the responding poet Jonathan Aaron here turns to the matter of linguistic collage, telling of the genesis of the generic title, and pseudonym as well, that Schwitters contrived for a series of works. He alludes in the poem to *Merkur*—the German word for Mercury—and, in "four sevenths of the German word for pain" to the way in which the word *Merz*, chopped out of *Kommerz* ("commerce"), is also *Schmerz* ("pain") minus its *Sch-*. (It might be further observed that minus its *m* it would be *Scherz*, or "joke.")

Aaron's poem gathers up, in its loose, free-verse quatrains, the bits and pieces of the collage that on "a closer look" yield up their individual natures, their sources in parts of objects in the outside world. They become "Aphorisms for the eye / framed in snatches of an exploded grammar"—alluding possibly to the syntactic, lexical, and phonemic explosions in Schwitters's own verse, and certainly to the stuttering and scattered syntax of the reorganized fragments in this particular collage.

But what emerges toward the end, when the poem has collected its observations of the bits and pieces, comes from recollection, of an image the poet has seen previously outside of the frame of the piece itself. It is a vision of the artist himself in the unexploded grammar of a landscape, conventionally picturesque, but yet in exile. JH

Prayer

William Logan

on a sculpture by Georg Kolbe

The spirit of the rough air, cast in bronze,
kneels naked on the gallery's wooden floor,
a fallen girl of fallen Babylons,
an ancient insect trapped in amber ore.

When Coleridge walked the high lake's shadowed fell
talking of God's unchristian love of man
or what excuses Adam made in hell,
he knew no more of prayer than men can.

Like Eve, each woman tastes a man's desire
more by the reputation of the tongue
and chooses for herself what men require,
the evil and the good, the old and young.

Love left a trace in its apocrypha.
Like Eve before her, she was born to please.
Now taking off her panties and her bra,
she opens her mouth, and then goes down on her knees.

Georg Kolbe
(German, 1887–1947)

Kneeling Woman (Kniende), 1926
Bronze
54.6 x 23 x 20 cm
Bruce B. Dayton, B.A. 1940, and Director's Funds
1967.63
© 2001 Artists Rights Society (ARS), New York / VG Bild-Kunst, Bonn

Georg Kolbe started his artistic career as a draftsman. Studying first in Dresden and then in Munich, he joined the Julian Académie in Paris for several years. During this time, he was influenced by Auguste Rodin after a visit to the French sculptor's studio. After 1898, he turned completely to sculpture while studying in Rome. Returning to Germany, he worked with Max Klinger in Leipzig. After the First World War, Kolbe became a professor and then a member of the Akademie der Kunst in Berlin. Although he explored Cubism in sculpture, his predominantly bronze sculptural work is linked to his drawings of the female figure. Kolbe's *Kneeling Woman* combines the immediacy of Degas's wax sculptures with Rodin's physicality. JW

Kolbe's kneeling figure does not look to be praying. Her gaze is not so much averted *from* some kind of presence as rather directed *at* the ground, a virtual ground that is not, in fact, the flat surface on which the whole bronze piece stands. Nevertheless, the poet here construes her genuflection in an ironic and complex way, linking this young woman to Eve, and thereby to a version of the *Ewigweiblichen*—Faust's "eternal feminine." The opening line—"The spirit of the rough air cast in bronze"—seems to point to matters of sculptural form, specific posture, and active surface. It leaves open the question, too, of the significance of such a spirit's being trapped in its materialization in bronze, as if that were a fall in itself. The question of prayer comes in obliquely, in the second stanza, with the implication that prayer, and perhaps the particular posture and gesture of the figure itself, must be feminine.

The controlled tone of this poem, distant but speculatively engaged, is in good part controlled by the rhymed pentameter quatrains and simple but fairly high level of diction, until the last line. There, the rhythm provided by the additional syllables, and the hinted wordplay of the modern colloquial "go down on," help to close off the aphoristic observations with something close to a punchline. JH

Argument from Design

Paul Kane

> Tell them, dear, that if eyes were made for seeing,
> Then Beauty is its own excuse for being.
>
> —Emerson

Imagine a tea and coffee set
          (of cleanest, simplest design)
                   on a silver-banded tray.
Imagine a family of four
          (father, mother, daughter, son)
                   bound in a magic circle.

(i)

The ideal form is designed for use
     and when used up, the ideal remains.
     A pattern, a surface, explains
itself: being is its own excuse.

No need here for the signature mark
     when every object has its aura—
     unique, undying, like Aurora
(not Tithonus, art's heresiarch).

Style is become a lexicon, yet
     art is craft when craft is art—"Design
     Art" you call it, finer than Fine:
ideal *and* real (poet turns profit).

Take a line, a curve, spiral, circle...
     take the elements of form—motifs
     drawn on a well of beliefs—
and make the simple most masterful.

(ii)

"You could not evade me, having spent all
those hours dusting and polishing the past.
I left my mark on you, as you on me—
this little dent, that careless scratch and scrape.
Did we ever take tea together? Or,
did I sit in the corner admired
until you came to me and held me close?

You see what shape I'm in now. We tarnish
with time, lines deepen, the substrate yellow.
But you recognized my picture right off
in that book? And here we are together.
Happy chance! (Though chance always feels fated.)
Why treat me with kid gloves—or cotton ones?
Take them off, touch me, feel my cool smoothness.
I was made to handle, though few could look
without emotion. I was special then,
and am officially so now. I've found
my place at last—though why the family
got rid of me I'll never understand.
Too much trouble, a little too classy?
At least they kept me together, else I'd
fall to pieces. You talk for awhile now,
I want to hear your voice, hear it echo
within me. No? Well then our time is up.
Will you remember me to the others?
Tell them I'm every bit the same as when...
Tell them I'm well here, surrounded by such
interesting types—a whole gallery.
What? Am I reflected in your eyes?
Listen, we are all objects of desire."

(iii)

Coffee Pot

You stand over the others, your stature
undisputed, though the dark and even
bitter cup you offer cannot be given
to all guests. That's where the children's rapture

comes in, the one full of laughter and charm,
the other, lovely, pouring forth kindness.
Still, amelioration isn't blindness,
and the mother, also strong, means no harm

when she stands, not quite in opposition
(your aims are too similar for that) but
wholly as herself—seeking to disrupt
what she won't countenance or envision.

Always on your mettle, the blood can start
at the very sight of you, the pulse race
when seated before you face-to-face:
with designs upon us, you affect the heart.

Tea Pot

Ritual is design: that ceremony
each morning—a dish of tea, a biscuit,
the glass doors open to the balcony.
        Steeping, the tea pot puts a lid on despair.

In a mural above the bed, St. Andrew
listens to the fish, as we watch to catch
a glimpse of how to understand you.
        Steeping, the tea pot puts a lid on despair.

What moves below the flowing surface
remains mysterious. Depths are deceiving
and the bowl, aquamarine, thwarts our purpose.
        Steeping, the tea pot puts a lid on despair.

Once, the mask slipped and the pain, apparent,
made a mirror of our gaze and shamed us.
Now we work to acquire what we thought inherent.
        Weeping, the tea pot put a lid on despair.

Creamer

Most open, most vulnerable—in a glance
you apprise of good fortune or mischance.

No one suffers quite like a daughter,
who, in unalloyed joy, is the author

of herself: the milk separate from the cream.
But this knowledge is dark—as though some dream.

To play your part you must know your place
and give everything over to efface

what you are: a silver vessel, not full,
not empty, but whole, graceful, never null.

Sugar Bowl

How you sweated that day in the heat!
Your shirt clung to your back in fear.
You shook with a fever that scared us.
What shook you would kill you next year.

Crystallized, hardened, you never lost
the sweetness that everyone loved.
A little of you went a long way.
When the push came, you knew to shove.

Your two sides showed in symmetry,
as if holding you took both hands.
You kept up appearances, kept your
distance: only withdrawal withstands.

Who could have borne all that promise
without thinking failure a crime?
You doled out grains from sugar cubes
as if hoarding the sands of time.

Tray

You house and embrace them,
the ideal image of the perfect
family—imperfections and all.
Who cares if the brass pins
holding you aren't original?
The home you came from,
an organic thing, with the defect
of its vertu—its blemished beauty—grew,
flowered, went to seed, to its origins.
It was not built to last, but to renew.
Like a tray, serving its purpose,
it held a family, and it moved us
to embrace and house you.

(iv)

Why did you select this piece?
    We were standing by the gravesite
    and the wind was in the spruce trees.

How well did you know the artist?
    A bell rang in the middle of the night
    and I climbed a flight of stairs.

Is this poem biographical?
    When we planted the garden
    the wild phlox stood round.

Why don't you answer these questions?
    Imagine a tea and coffee set
    bound in a magic circle.

Ilonka Karasz
(American, born Hungary, 1896-1981)

For Paye and Baker Manufacturing Company, (American, 1891–ca. 1935)
Tea and Coffee Service, North Attleboro, Massachusetts, ca. 1928
Electroplated nickel silver, bakelite, Coffee Pot: H. 17.2 cm, Teapot: H. 12.3 cm
Sugar Bowl: H. 9.1, DIAM. 10.2 cm, Cream Pitcher: H. 5.1 cm, Tray: H. 2.9 cm, DIAM. 30.5 cm
M. Josephine Dial in memory of Gregory T. Dial, B.S. 1930, Fund.
1985.1.1-5

The Hungarian Ilonka Karasz studied design at the Royal School of Arts and Crafts in Budapest before emigrating to the United States in 1913. Karasz herself used this set until her death in 1981. A photograph of the set was published in Paul Frankl's seminal book *Form and Reform* (1930) and is an important example of purist Bauhaus aesthetic applied to the so-called industrial arts. JW

The title of this suite of poems (appropriate to a suite or set of objects) is from William James's account of a mode of inferring the existence of a Creator from the observable facts of the world. Here, "Design" refers to the art of craft, as well as to the craft of art—the word means drawing, planning, intending, as well as specifically to the *objets de virtù*—rather than painting or sculpture—dealt with in the poem. Its epigraph, from Emerson's "The Rhodora," plays ambivalently about the matter of craft-as-art.

In this case, a silver service by Ilonka Karasz is the object of interpretive consideration. (Karasz was also known for her *New Yorker* covers in the 1940s; questions of her possible connection with the poet seem to arise, and are pointedly unanswered, at the end of the poem.) The way they are taken and what is made of them are both like and unlike the way that painted versions of themselves in a still-life might be, and the poet keeps making his point about their being objects of actual, although luxurious, use. Kane's verse glistens with puns as brilliant as the surfaces of the pieces it addresses ("Am I reflected in your eyes? / Listen, we are all objects of desire" or, in craft vs. art, "'Design/ Art' you call it, finer than Fine: / ideal *and real* (poet turns profit))." As the sequence continues, in (ii) the whole service speaks its own blank-verse monologue, followed by various verse schemes in which the various pieces in the set are addressed. The initial trope of the set as a family returns at the end of the lines speaking to the tray. JH

In Storage: A Calder Cat
Robert B. Shaw

Curious interlopers in our households,
they come and go. And when they go for good
the ones that oddly deigned to live with us
enter a tenth life of family legend,
or say of leitmotif, always beginning
"That was the one." That was the one who caught
a bat on the roof and brought it in the window.
That was the one who always swallowed string.
That was the one who died, sadly enough,
when a tinned ham slid off the kitchen counter.
Note how often the theme is appetite.
But this one? There's no tidbit to entice him.
Between svelte and scrawny, like some we've known,
able to appear both round and flat,
lolling with one nonchalant front paw
crossed on the other, but with ears a-cock,
the negligible peg of a tail perked up
assertively—as anyone can see,
his nose is out of joint. One is not moved
to pet that coat of what looks like scuffed umber
shoe polish rubbed over streaks and whorls
of wood graining that here stand in for stripes.
But see the eyes of this barn-timber idol.
Idol or Eye Doll? Bulging like a pair
of tethered blimps, those eyes return our stare,
triggering us to blink first, intimating
that *we* are the truant pupils come to take
instruction or correction in this sanctum
of storage cabinets, the inmost shrine.
Fresh from this pilgrimage, I'd recommend
this cat stay in the cupboard. He's not one
we can imagine willing to adopt us.
Homely, heraldic, too sedate to spit,
this wooden totem's scorn for us is total.
This is the one we wince to think of, watching
even after the metal door swings shut.

Alexander Calder
(American, 1898–1976)

Cat, ca. 1930
Wood
19.7 x 66.7 x 9.5 cm
Director's Purchase Fund
1967.42
© 2001 Estate of Alexander Calder/
Artists Rights Society (ARS), New York

This charming sculpture is indicative of Alexander Calder's early interest in animals and the whimsicality of their play. Trained as a mechanical engineer at the Strong Institute of Technology in Hoboken, New Jersey, he later enrolled in the Arts Students League in New York and began sketching sporting events and circus performances for the *National Police Gazette* in 1924. His first book of illustrations, *Animal Sketching* (1926), was based on his observations of animals in the New York zoos. In the late 1920s Calder went to Paris and studied at the Académie de la Grande Chaumière. During his Paris stay, he was drawn to the work of Joan Miró and Paul Klee. At this time, he also began creating a miniature circus (1926–32, now at the Whitney Museum), which he hand-operated in small performances. *Cat* is from this period and reflects Calder's skills of observation and in handling the wood to capture the cat's expression.
JW

This poem starts out in the first eleven lines as a meditation on felinity—and on our own discourse about it—in general. We might feel that it is evading its own interpretive responsibility about a work of art by mistaking it for a purely transparent presentation of a "subject" (here, a cat). But then with the fine device of including a question, he begins an ecphrastic reading of Calder's sculpture, addressing appropriate questions of form and surface as well as those of anatomical detail. (Painting and drawing cats frequently presents the fascinating problem of dealing at once with the way their bodily forms become generalized under their skins, and the way in which their markings interrupt that generality of surface. In this case, the literal flattening of a carved piece introduces a different agenda for the inquiring eye.) But then the poet audaciously considers an accidental aspect of his encounter with the carving—it had been kept by the Art Gallery in a closed locker, in which the poet viewed it—and subsumes it into the matter of the piece itself.

Shaw plays on his poetic instrument of elegant blank-verse lines to produce a tone at once formal and colloquial. And after its strategy of including the carved cat among the almost clichéd catalogue of anecdotal ones he comes down, at the end ("this wooden totem's scorn for us is total") to reaffirming the way in which the sculptured piece embodies emblematically and totally one traditional characterization of feline-human relations which is never really "total" in personal actuality. JH

The Phantom Cart
By Salvador Dalí, 1933

Martha Hollander

What a confection!
A caramel desert softly browned
under the butterscotch sky.
Close by, a fragment of pottery
as lacy as a cookie skates
headlong into the morning sun.
The pioneers' covered wagon
moves toward the horizon, its wheels
are poised in the creamy sand like toothpicks,
moving towards a little city
sunk in the sand like a brave
clump of walnuts in custard.

Where is the horse that draws the load,
whose three legs so sweetly tread the ground?
And what is that in the cart itself?
Two people, it seems, parent and child,
the larger stiff-shouldered,
the smaller, pert as a pawn.
Or are they both spires in the city beyond,
framed in an empty wagon
and topped with domes like cherries?
How do you know if the one beside you
is only a far-off shell, architect's dream?
How to be sure that the great figure
sprawling over your present life
(so full of mess and banter and ferocious
love under the implacable profile)
is in fact a shape of the future?

The only way to know is to get
ahead of the cart, to churn through
the retarding sugar of the desert
and turn back to peer under the canopy.
And what about entering the city itself,
robed in a cooling sauce of blue?
Otherwise there is no depth,
only a crowd of delicious shapes

to grab and savor, like the
child-guards on apartment windows,
laying a black roadmap on the
yellow-gray family of oblongs
that mark local bridges and towers.
You have to focus and refocus constantly,
allowing the grid of the summer screen
to overcome the landscape.
Or to recede into the afternoon,
bound for the next thing?
The only way to know is to grow up.

Salvador Dalí
(Spanish, 1904–89)

The Phantom Cart, 1933
Oil on panel
15.9 x 20.3 cm
Gift of Thomas F. Howard
1953.51.1
© 2001 Kingdom of Spain, Gala-Salvador Dalí Foundation /
Artists Rights Society (ARS), New York

Here, almost floating in a sea of disturbing yellow, two people and a precarious cart seem frozen in the landscape, approaching the distant village. The scale of the cart, village, and landscape appear monumental (in spite of the small scale of the painting). A thing, like discarded litter, sits in the lower left-hand corner; it shows something old and destroyed, and its haunting presence here shatters the dream that one can move back in time and repair the past. This fragment is not grounded or stable, but it has a shadow and therefore inescapable density. But the meaning of the painting is found in the title—the cart is not a cart, but a phantom cart. JW

The fact that, in this case, the poet is also a professional art historian (though working in Dutch art of the seventeenth century) provides an interesting aspect of this poem which becomes highlighted at its very end. The poet got to know Salvador Dalí's tiny painting of a metamorphic vision—seen through the rear opening of a covered wagon—of a distant city whose rising buildings pun visually on the wagon's riders seen from behind when she was an undergraduate at Yale, and with what was probably a more naive view of Dalí and his problematic oeuvre than she would eventually acquire. But the original magic of the painting for the younger viewer is slightly dimmed for the later one in the metaphor of a highly constructed dessert introduced at the beginning of the poem. The three free-verse strophes or stanzas present an almost classic structure for a pictorial meditation: first, a formal ecphrasis, or description of what is seen; next, a series of questions, directed to the scene itself (only the cherries having wandered in from the first strophe), raising at its end the matter of past, present, and future. The final strophe gives a kind of figurative answer to the last questions asked, dwelling on time past and on futurity, and pointing obliquely, although in its direct final line, to the maturing of sensibility and wisdom in the poet's own ecphrastic gaze. JH

Dialogue
Karl Kirchwey

Alberto Giacometti, *Hands Holding the Void*, 1934

What is the tablet at your knees?
　—The mirror where imitation dies.

What is the slot-eyed head that sleeps
on the angled bench, and slyly keeps
a ruminant's tongue for prophecy?
　—It dreams of the pure idolatry
　of imagination, its consummate solitude.

What have your breasts nourished, white with dread?
What grew in your belly after maidenhead?
What have your knees, sharp as new flints, grappled?
　—There is only the silence of my body,
　an emanation of desire itself,
　in its ignorance, to be loved and love.
　The prints of his hands are on me nowhere.

What is the mote that swims in your eye?
　—A sentimental uncertainty.
　Metastasis. The twinkling of the atom.
　Five barley loaves. Two fish. Capernaum.
　The broken Catherine wheel of thought.

What is the frame to which you are bound
on heavy casters, without a sound?
　—The three dimensions of loneliness:
　exile; memory; dread of the future.
　The velvet dark of infinite space.

What cry does your mouth form itself to utter?
　—An iron mask, each eye a louver,
　whether of knowledge or of appearance;
　something haughty, distracting, awkward,
　the troops wore at Argonne in the mud.
　That war and its eight million dead.

What, after all, then, are you like?
　—I efface the void with breasts, belly, knees.
　A metaphor finds its way through darkness.

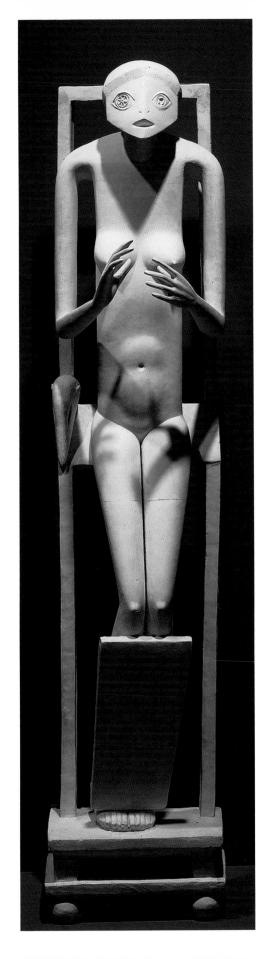

Reality awakens the eye,
but cannot be known except as detail
which makes the space of its own betrayal.
I live between obsession and will.

What do your hands shape, finally?
The ashes of some ancient story?
A predator fended off? Applause?
—On a stage I compose myself to speak,
for once to summon from hopelessness
a human object. To summon praise.

Alberto Giacometti
(Swiss, 1901–66)

Hands Holding the Void, 1934
Plaster
156.2 x 34.3 x 29.2 cm
Anonymous Gift
1950.730
© 2001 Artists Rights Society (ARS), New York / ADAGP, Paris

Holding the void, and perched on a ledge with a bird, the thin woman is held in this precarious position by kneeling. Here Giacometti pushes her in this uncomfortable position and exposes the vulnerability of her belly and breasts. The two different kinds of eyes glare out into our space seeking stability—stability which neither the material nor structure gives her. JW

The dialogue of the title of Kirchwey's poem is between the gazer and the piece of sculpture. But it is a very limited sort of dialogue, almost, in fact, a catechism, almost like that of the Greek Anthology poem by Posidippus mentioned earlier. In the older poem, the questioner merely elicits information from the statue of Occasion or Opportunity about, e.g., the name of its sculptor, or iconographic details ("Why does your hair hang over your face?"—"So someone who meets me can seize me by the forelock," etc.)

But Kirchwey's interrogation goes further and deeper. It seems very clear that the artist's own title has helped shape the poem's agenda. And the very way in which the questions it poses are framed privileges certain visual events in Giacometti's white plaster piece even as it seems blind to others. (The ambiguous elongated head of the rodent-like animal—some rodent? a greyhound or whippet?—below the figure's right elbow, for example, and the fact that the pupil of the right eye is a spoked wheel.)

With the third question, it becomes clear that the figure itself is being addressed and is answering, and not some outside authority. The poet has acknowledged that he had also been thinking about an interview with Giacometti by David Sylvester, a book by Matti Meged, and André Breton's *L'Amour Fou.* But the poem's interrogation is no interview, and what the poet makes the figure answer only raises more silent questions. JH

Conversation

Annie Finch

Edward Weston's *Squash*, 1936

"Delve for me, delve down, delve past your body, crowned
by its hidden stem, like a shadowy alarm;
see how you vanish past our dark-shed charm,
throat over throat, ankle to ankle, bound
in our different arches, summer-nicked and browned
interlocking rings in the chain of wrist and arm."

"Lie for me, lie. I want to feel you turn.
Mark out the summer's bending mouth and learn
to cradle the concrete ground till it softens. Stay.
Measure me past my stem. Though your shadows churn,
close yourself over. Encompass me like clay."

Edward Weston
(American, 1886–1958)

Squash, 1936
Gelatin silver print
19.3 x 24.4 cm
Gift of Charles Seymour, Jr., B.A. 1935
1964.62.1

Born in the suburbs of Chicago in 1886, Weston traveled often to Califor-
nia and then to New York City, where he met Alfred Stieglitz. Stieglitz's
Gallery 291 influenced his turn to abstraction in photography. Weston is
well known for his sensuous images of vegetables, particularly peppers,
which celebrate curves, echoing nudes, as well as the natural forms of
landscape. This image of two modest squashes nestled together to form a
full circle is a small still-life that conveys sensuality. Weston received the
first Guggenheim grant for photography, and he continued photographing
landscapes of the West and Southwest until 1958. JW

The "Conversation" here is not between the poet and the work of art as in other instances. Rather, it is between two elements in the photograph; and the very title suggests a generic status for the photographic image, as if pictures of two similar objects set side by side could show either rural or urban landscape elements, or two personages of some sort or other, whose relation was not so much structural or spatial but immediately perceived as narrative. The two squashes here must thus be doing something to one another through engagement or gesture, or, in this case, expressing that relation discursively. Finch here chooses the option of having her poem spoken *out of* the picture, but not to a viewer of it (and, simultaneously, a reader of the poem itself). Instead, the two personified squashes are engaged in a highly figurative "conversation" with each other (and the Latin root of "turn" lying hidden in that word, as resonant for a poet as the color of a shadow for a painter, emerges at the beginning of the larger, vertical squash's shorter reply to the recumbent one).

Each impersonating fruit speaks in a rhymed, five-beat stanza, and each marks in the other a gestural significance of its own from which we, as observers of the photograph, would be first to come to. What their discourse adds to our seeing is the result of what each of them sees in, and as, the other. JH

After a Sculpture by Sophie Taeuber-Arp

Tony Sanders

A
piece
of wood
in the shape
of a lemon except
for the fact the fruit is cut
cut into twice the left slice nearly
civilized as though the wedge were for a gin
and tonic or flounder one might guess
except for the fact that the broader
cut is double the size of the other
the idea of lemon in a drink turns
sour maybe just as perishable as
fruit for a   thought because a piece of wood
in the shape of one   lemon is a piece of wood turned
on a lathe or table or in the hands   of a sculptor who knows a body
knows how a body in spite of its fullness rises to pinnacle an apex turned
upside down surely akin to a top a kid's toy packed in an attic and uncovered
abandoned buried and unearthed in the woods except for the fact that a piece
of wood may not be fruit may not be a plain top spun into and out of oblivion
because the upturned cut might be a mouth opened in awe at some sun or sky
in the manner of a child one innocent
apparently uplifted by a patch of light
after so much darkness so much pain
in contrast to the gaping maw below
epitome of hunger much too strong
to reflect feeling since God knows
there cannot be feeling after abuse
as in the case of mythieal a figure
Kaspar Hauser who endures as a
gnome half real half conjured up
born in borne out of the world
it is always hard to distinguish
between relief and surrender
O inanimate object unable to see I see
in you elements of many of us bound
up in contradictions twin eyeless half
faces forming a sober portrait at last I
understand the difference between the
off-balance life and death of an orphan
and the equipoise of a wood sculpture

Sophie Taeuber-Arp was born in Switzerland, where she studied textile
design, which she in turn taught in Zurich from 1916–29. It is during this
time that she met Hans Arp and became an active participant in Zurich's
Dada movement. From 1927 to 1928 she worked with her husband and
Theo van Doesburg on the interior decoration of the Café Audette in
Strasbourg, France (destroyed during the Second World War). In the
1930s, the couple moved to Paris and remained in contact with Dadaism.
At this time, she turned away from geometric shapes and explored
circular forms. Working with objects in the round, she often chose
wood to choreograph the interaction of multiple dimensions in her
sculpture. Through the traditional skill of wood-turning, Taeuber-Arp
transformed this piece of wood into an engaging and charming shape,
reminiscent of a chess piece, a knight's head armor, or a gnome's head
where the material, wood, is tamed. Here the wood grain is integral to her
composition and its unpainted surface becomes its color. As Marcel
Duchamp wrote in his original text for the Société Anonyme's 1950
catalogue, "Sophie Taeuber-Arp, in her attitude of detachment about
herself as an artist, reminds us of the anonymous artisan of the Middle-
Ages." JW

A poetic reading of a piece of abstract art will often tend to read nonrepresentational forms as signs nonetheless, starting from what a formal structure or relation or transition might "look like." Adducing such visual similes variously may or may not be inappropriate to a nonpoetic "reading" of the work in question. But for language, full of desire to embrace and contain a purely visual formulation, every work of art is something of a mirror. This poem is full of awareness of such interpretive dangers, and one cannot assume that reading the two cuts in the form as mouths is all there is to the matter. Sanders's shaped or "pattern" poem employs a mode that goes back to Hellenistic Greek poetry (and best known from the poems of George Herbert, Guillaume Apollinaire, May Swenson, and others). Its format creates a silhouette of an object or sign generated by lines of type, whose length and placement it then employs as a verse form. In this case, the silhouetted representation causes the cuts in the wood to appear as voids.

Brooding on what the prior condition—before being perhaps painfully cut and polished—of the piece's block of wood might have been, the poet thinks of Kaspar Hauser, the famous early-nineteenth-century boy brought up in a dark cellar and without language until the age of sixteen, when he was educated and restored to social life. JH

Bonnard

Rosanna Warren

It's like this: three large slices of
      world split into smaller, pulpy
            fistfuls of world within each

world-slice, and it all hurts, so
      debonair, so juicy: where
            is the woman, after all, the

center of this story? Well, we are
      mistaken. The center
            is a pillar of wrong

light, gone smooshed and over-ripe, re-
      flected, glassed, and we
            should be included but

we're not. It's not our house. The light
      doesn't smash us
            in the face or tilt

us backwards out of our lives. Still,
      the column of garden
            hardly holds the story

together, and pomegranate seeds
      spill loose across the tiles and up
            the door post. So

many mirrors, you'd think, would give
      a point of view. They don't.
            They just ferment

sunlight into three species
      of jam. The seeds
            of light will stick

in our teeth, the paste of light
      wedge, unswallowed, in
            our throats. A flame

spurts in the toothy grate, but the soul
      stays dark. She's bent, the
            soul, steeped in her confiture

of shadows; leans naked, bruised,
      peripheral, half-
            erased. She's trying

to pray. She's trying to wash.
      She's shivering in
            cold. She has understood

that never, in this life, will she be clean.

Pierre Bonnard
(French, 1867–1947)

Interior at Le Cannet, 1938
Retouched 1943
Oil on canvas
126.4 x 125.1 cm
The Katharine Ordway Collection
1980.12.19
© 2001 Artists Rights Society (ARS), New York / ADAGP, Paris

The theme of his bathing wife, Marthe de Méligny, is a leitmotif in many of Pierre Bonnard's paintings. The particular moment of his wife emerging from the bathtub allows Bonnard to juxtapose decorative interior space that celebrates pattern and spatial relationship broken up by light and color. Bonnard worked on several different paintings at once, and often tucked colors for the different compositions into other canvases. This method accounts for his extremely rich and varied use of colors. JW

It is not surprising that the poet Rosanna Warren, who as an undergraduate at Yale majored in painting before becoming a poet and literary scholar, should have chosen a work by so very painterly an artist as Bonnard. Indeed, her poem is simply entitled with the artist's name, as if it reported a confrontation with a whole way of painting. The one question, toward the opening, is about the woman inferred from a trace of her in the painting (the left arm and hand of a figure facing forward but blocked by the brightly lit mirrored wall). It is not an inquiry into the picture's possible narrative, but of another sort of compositional and structural "story"—acutely non-narrative in the usual sense—of what holds the painting together. Warren's poem abandons all mimetic concerns save for its own, even as it speaks literally and allegorically at once: "So // many mirrors, you'd think, would give / a point of view. They don't."

In the poem's free-verse tercets—systematically indented so that the longest extent of the stanza's last line is roughly 30–35 picas from the beginning of the first one—the lines are very heavily enjambed. This allows an observation such as "Still, / the column of garden / hardly holds the story // together . . ." which is about both the structure of the painting and the coherence of the writer's apprehension of it, to seem to invoke the necessary architectonic coherence of the poem itself. JH

Lexington Avenue Subway, 1941

J. D. McClatchy

after Walker Evans

And on the way to somewhere else—
he can't think of the stop, the stops
are quiet, strangers turning in the light—
he's leaned back against the window,
against the glazed leaves, the chips
of seablue and skygold, the platform's
map of boundaries the rain changes
while through the grate the upper world,
on its own iron wheels, is sidetracked
towards history's fenced-in yard, and shut
his eyes to imagine that, years from now,
he is sitting beside himself, the dream's
train of thought pulling the figure forward
from all the disappointments. There he is.
He'll ask this nerveless dark angel of age
again what he did, what he did wrong.

How could you know what your father
would never admit, what your mother
would never accept? How could you know
their own fears were your child-bed,
your small, high window onto the city?
The unwelcome advice, the useless clarity,
the small passions, how confusing
all the ideas of others turned out to be.
The woman you married, the other men
she came to love more, the only son
you haven't seen because he wanted any life
but the one you gave him to throw away....
The parts have been worked out for us,
and you pause, as if by accident,
and try to recall just what it was
she said in the doorway. Was she angry?

Capturing two men's moment of quiet in the noisy subway, Evans used his photographic skills to give stillness to his work. For his series of New York City subway photographs, taken over a period of twenty-five years, Walker rode the subway incognito, carrying a small camera hidden in his vest, while documenting ordinary street life. In 1966, Evans published eighty-nine of these photographs (including this one) in a book entitled *Many Are Called*. This loaded title is taken from Christ's words in the Gospels: "Many are called, but few are chosen," possibly referring to Evans's tight editing of thousands of photographs for this one volume. By making these everyday scenes into photographic objects, Evans records the dignity that resides in daily routine. He was a professor of photography at Yale after 1965 and died in New Haven in 1975. JW

A photograph can always elicit the kind of interpretive question that a painting or drawing will not—not so much, "what does this picture mean?" but rather, more concretely, "what was happening in front of the lens at precisely the time it was taken that resulted in this image, here, now?" A poem will frequently cut the Gordian knot of such speculation. J. D. McClatchy does not brood about whether these two dozing figures were traveling companions or merely fellow travelers. Instead his poem *knows* what they are, and he starts with a certain statement, which only then is followed by questioning. The figures are a young man (the "he") of the narrated first stanza of sixteen unrhyming lines, and a shadowy but substantial older version of himself, the "dark angel of age" who speaks the italicized lines of the second one.

What might have been an outside narrator's traditional opening interrogation of the whole photograph becomes internalized in the questioning mode of the second stanza, and interpretive uncertainties reappear—in the reading not of images, but of life itself—with the ambiguous reference of the "she" and the unrecallable "what it was / she said in the doorway." And finally, the matter of the almost naive ecphrastic question ("Do these people know each other?"), avoided originally in this poem, returns with our realization that the young man on the right cannot know the other personage is there; the older one, looking down and inwardly, knows all too much about the other, a presence of his own past.

JH

Head

Peter Sacks

Simply to hold back the fraying stem, bud, scale, blur, wing, tooth,
eye-flecked water that will burn before the other signs give way,

earth-beaten, carved into the single root—your eyes now looking back
at white-shelled sockets—shadow ships drowned out to carry their

own cargo stripped & haunted here—a search?—a harvest?—
wind comes over us unsung if not for other sounds—ancestral—

laboring—the memory of river-water—blades of quick attention
led away—that battleground you fasten over you—your skull, your face

of fiber hearing it if you can listen far enough—
there is a continent before the gods, there is a door of bone

between—behind you now the field is opening its jaws
below the ridge—there is no hollowness through which this whispering

can fall—no peace-filled re-imagining—now it is yours, repaid,
a monument through which no birdcalls seep—

you have to see it here, the place reserved for craft, for prayer,
in which you pause unknowing so these pieces of the tree—

not life, not replication—grow around us, thickening, however
much we cut them back, the branches of black ivory, the leaves

that open elsewhere to descend, ungatherable, around another generation's
thirst for everything between itself & its own end—do not

come home, they say, begin again, take all the time that's left, take Africa.

Unknown artist

Lutumbo Iwa Kindi Image
Lega Civilization, Northeastern Democratic Republic of Congo
20th century
Ivory, cowrie shells
14.9 x 7.4 x 10.1 cm
 Gift of Mr. and Mrs. James M. Osborn for the Linton Collection of African Art
1964.76.21

The Lega people live in a forest region and aspire to moral authority by gaining high rank in the *Bwami* initiation rites, of which *Kindi* is the highest rank. This object is a *Kindi* piece and *Kindi* members use small ivory sculptures such as this one as emblems, depicting moral perfection. Here the smooth surface is equated with calm and wisdom, and the cowrie shells used for eyes indicate heightened vision acquired through successive initiations. JW

A poem of a century ago, or a very naive one of our own day, might seek to invoke the matter of "Africa" by crude means: pounding accentual rhythms, anaphora, some mode of conceptual minimalism. In Sacks's poem, the couplets of long, unmeasured lines frame another sort of rhythm, one in which disconnected, paratactic images and coherent though unpunctuated indicative sentences serve as contrasting rhythmic elements on another scale from those of syllable, stress, or printed line length. The ecphrastic tone is one of a resolving bewilderment. The head seems to be speaking in the second and third couplets and to return ambiguously here and there later on in the course of the gazing speaker's questions and assertions, and to partake in the almost mutual realization that "there is a door of bone / between us."

The poet himself, like the head, comes originally from Africa, although his native cosmopolitan city of Durban in South Africa is a far cry from the Democratic Republic of Congo (formerly Zaire), just as his implicit story of the head as he confronts it in a museum is wildly distant from the material tale of its cultural and historical identity and function. Sacks seeks to place the object in a unique sort of imaginative site, "the place reserved for such unknowing," and hearing no speech but "residual whisperings." It is through such acknowledgments that the poem arrives at the final and most metaphorical injunction (is it of the leaves?) to "take Africa." JH

A Shape in Two Minds

Regarding
Marcel Duchamp's
In advance of the broken arm

George Bradley

gorgeous things had fallen
all night fallen for centuries
and you dug down to clean
space in which to think first
through repeated presence
any spit and image of itself

de
ep
next through the geometric
solid obstruction line forms
beneath dimension drawn
under blanket of approved
perspective and its uniform
icon of stormy air apparent

de
ep
er
hi
you swept texture smooth
as ice brushed substance
aside stroke at one stroke
discarded sent up to right
and left your way relieved
of decorous accumulation

de
ep
er
hi
gh
er
with so little left you pushed
past attraction the very idea
scraped to this level absent
of least lingering or leftover
hue anaesthetic alpenglow
sought the irreducible zero

de
ep
er
hi
gh
er
de
ep
with the base grown visible
at last and the likeness you
had never liked to start with
vanished these two remain
instrument and swath route
and road a tool's exhibition

de
ep
er
hi
gh
er
de
ep
er
hi
this path made plain before
you a deprived and analytic
purity of the absurd a comic
dignity one firmly grounded
profoundly obvious starkest
non-plussed ultra oh and 0

d e e p
e r
h i g h
 er
 de
 ep
 er
 hi
 gh
 er
 de
 ep
 er
when all revelation's object
is bedrock and crystal clear
there is nothing to be done
but fill excavations thought
has made allowing beauty
to heap up let it snow let it

Marcel Duchamp
(French, 1887–1968)

In advance of the broken arm (Snow Shovel),
1945, replica of lost work of 1915
Wood and galvanized iron snow shovel
121.3 x 46.3 x 12.7 cm
Gift of Katherine S. Dreier to the Collection Société Anonyme
1946.99
© 2001 Artists Rights Society (ARS), New York /
ADAGP, Paris / Estate of Marcel Duchamp

Duchamp's first Readymade of 1915 consisted of a New York hardware
store snow shovel, which he then signed. Yale's *In advance of a broken
arm* of 1945 is a replica of the lost work of 1915. Duchamp purposefully
chose a functional object and believed that by endowing it with a title, the
artist would elevate the ordinary simply by isolating it through language.
By signing ordinary objects, he elevated the so-called found object into a
work of art. Through this ironic trick, Duchamp modified the very
definitions of art and challenged the notion of the artist as maker. Here
the title anticipates a mishandling of the snow shovel that can lead to
harm, a broken arm. The playfulness of these Readymades brings humor
to the world of high art. JW

Duchamp's Readymade—as the ordinary objects which he turned into works of art merely by exhibiting them as, and proclaiming them to be such, are called—is a mere snow shovel. Or perhaps, since for neither an artist nor a poet anything is ever merely "mere," we might say that it is about a snow shovel. Even as the title of the piece directs us toward one consequence of its careless use, George Bradley's "pattern poem" broods on the falling snow that will deepen as it piles higher ("high" and "deep" being also two qualities of the romantic poetic "Sublime") but is different from some of the other iconically formatted poems in this volume in that it changes its "shape" in successive stanzas to suggest a topsy-turvy sort of snow burial, with the handle covered in snow and only the blade emerging gradually with each six-line "dig" of the blade. Only at the end is the whole handle uncovered. But to get there the poem has had to work through an intense meditative consideration of the significance of such easily ordinary notions as pushing, scraping, shoveling, uncovering, and revealing—of snow and "instrument and swath route" and, throughout, of "the excavations thought / has made allowing beauty to heap up." At the same time, the poem keeps turning over and over the snowy matter of image and idea, of object and representation, and all the while, the more abstract matter of work and its nature as well. JH

Jackson Pollock's 13A: Arabesque
David R. Slavitt

A big mother, which is to say expensive,
it demands a big wallet, a big wall.
For a doodle, a slopping and dripping, on awning cloth,
an imposition of will even more than of talent?
My kid could do that, or my chimpanzee if I had one!
Well, let them think so and still shell out, big time.

The American art form is self-promotion.
Fame is the game. And Jackson's was solid: Jack
the Dripper. Not even Warhol's soup cans or Johns's
flags could match in shock value Pollock's defiance
of pretty pictures. You hang on a wall something useless
and expensive to show you believe in your taste—these squiggles
in housepainter's enamel, the tracks of a drunken
figure skater, an attempt at randomness
that fails as intelligence reasserts itself.

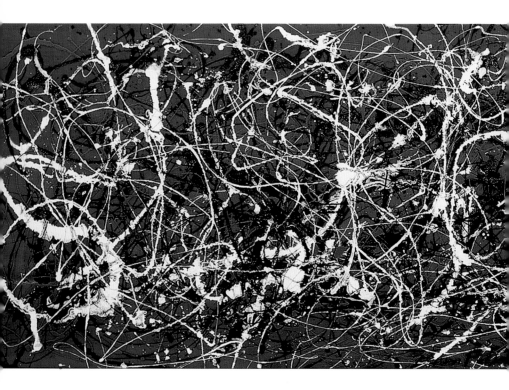

(His or our own?) Those glints are an artifact
of the glossy paint catching at random the light
of the installation. Up close, they go away.
And "Arabesque"? (Why not? The *"Lavender Mist"*
has no lavender in it, or mistiness either.)
Spatters, drips, outpourings. An inspired drunk,
a galoot, he was, with a dash, just, of refinement,
a guy smug sons of bitches could patronize
but pay just the same, through the nose, through every pore,
bleeding money.

　　　　But what America gives
she charges for. The convertible crashes, and there,
at the end of the road, in glistening viscous red
are his eloquent signature spatters—his action painting,
the stupid but shrewd intuitive gesture by which
he would keep his art's market healthy for years.

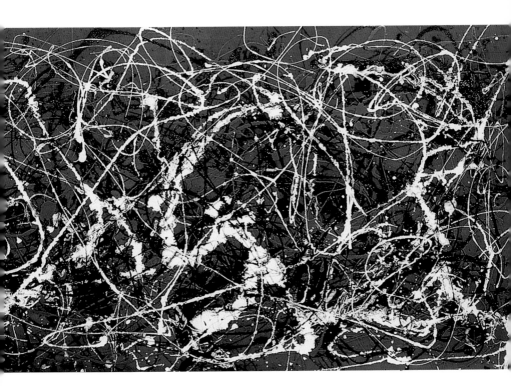

This elegant painting of drip enamel and oil, painted by Jackson Pollock on stained brown canvas, is self-contained. The pattern of figure eights reflects self-control, in spite of the seemingly facile mode of painting which this painting epitomizes. Pollock's drip paintings disrupt and challenge the Western tradition of painting and account for new ground being broken. By his shifting of the picture plane using industrial materials, he mediates between the worlds of domestic and artistic painting. His drip patterns—where the paint becomes blobby surface—challenge ways of understanding the role of paint. Likewise, by never putting the paintbrush on the canvas, he revolutionized the role of the painter's hand in the making of paintings. JW

In the case of this painting, the poet prefers not to deal with the formal agenda of Pollock's painting, nor with its uniqueness among his works of the period, but rather to deal with issues of reception, and with the painting as a token in the entrepreneurial energies of what was only beginning to become what has been known since as the "art world." One hears throughout the poem, couched in unrhymed, loose pentameter lines, a kind of ambivalence, alternating clichés of philistine reaction with detailed observation that might or not undermine them. The poet shows his own hand, though, in speaking of "an attempt at randomness / that fails as intelligence reasserts itself. / (His or our own?)." Although formally relatively chaste among Pollock's paintings of the period, the writer here implicitly takes the critical term "gestural" as applied to certain kinds of painting at the time and expands upon it to include gestures of expression, of manifesto, of several modes of self-promotion (the painting itself, its very mode, the artist's own), of the declarative stance of a kind of *machismo*, of various sorts of false or inauthentic connoisseurship in the world to which the painting was presented. In any event, Slavitt, seeming to deny that it may itself be one of Pollock's "pretty pictures," sees the painting as continuing to hold a declarative stance that commands a world to continue to look at it, whether that world can really see or not. JH

Rooms by the Sea
John Hollander

It may recall
An earlier glimpse of emptiness, a corner
Of a room by the sea, opening seemingly
Onto an uncontainable expanse of ocean.

The Front Room

To step right out of the room in to the sea
Directly, as if the land outside had all vanished with some
    silent *"Boom!"*
How wonderfully sudden it would be!

How grandly liberating it could be,
Having swept away all but sunlight with a painter's broom,
To step wide out of the room out to the sea,

To step straight out of the room onto the sea,
The blue hardwood floor or its surface stretched over
    an almost bottomless gloom:
How shockingly stabilizing it should be.

How nonchalant yet stirring it might be
Straw-hatted, wearing some buttonhole in yellow
    bloom,
To step gaily out of the room off to the sea.

To step wrongly out of the room up to the sea,
As if suddenly there were nothing any more about perspective that
    we could assume,
How seemingly possible, yet it can't be…

How simple and familiar it shall be
In the broadly ordinary that for the time being remains our doom
To step simply out of the room and down to the sea.

The Back Room

There are two kinds of rumor, like two sorts
Of space: one furnished with incident,
The other bare of detail, but booth full
Of inference, the silent hearsay of presence
And even of memory. And so of the two of
Us: the first, from all you know of it, empty
Of anything but sunlight casting
Its own unoccluded shadows —-
Sharp, bright—faintly shadowed themselves
In the alluding telltale spill of light on my back wall.
Outside its door there is no room
For anything but sea; inside there is no
Door by only a way to see into something
Of me—something about me—from your way of being
In something of the other room.
—And perhaps, too, in something of a quandary,
Looking into both us, for which of us
Is more private a place: it, all whispering of things?
Or my self, furnished with couch, dresser and—to confirm
Their substantiality—a picture of something
(But of what, and what else I have here in me,
Is for me to know and you never to find out)
And which more public?
I am furnished with memories—or, rather, souvenirs?—
No matter, I am full of the past, while its present
Openness to all of itself,
Even to me, looks always, too, to be looking out
Toward what is so grandly out There, the tremendous next thing
Which is all of the future you can, at best, foresee.

Edward Hopper
(American, 1882–1967)

Rooms by the Sea, 1951
Oil on canvas
73.7 x 101.9 cm
Bequest of Stephen Carlton Clark, B.A. 1903
1961.18.29

In the 1930s, Hopper and his wife built a house in Truro, Cape Cod, Massachusetts. The view of the bay from this simple house inspired the subject matter of this painting. Here the intensity of light and surreal presence of the sea at the open door juxtapose a stable, calm domestic interior with the impossibility of escaping to the outdoors and therefore transform these two rooms into a cul-de-sac trapping its inhabitants. JW

The epigraph here is from the author's own previous poem on another canvas of Hopper's (*Sun in an Empty Room*) in which he refers to the present painting. This later poem considers the rooms in two separate sections. The first considers the front, outer room, direct in the almost melodramatic precipitousness of the presence of the sea, and the almost flamboyantly characteristic geometric spill of yellow light on the floor and walls (the one to which a less prominent spill in the back room will be seen to "allude"). What we see of the front room is empty of all save for the doorknob and latch, and the two views into sea and sky beyond it, and a narrower chamber behind it. "The Front Room" turns the two halves of a thought over and over again, rhyming always on the words "sea" and "room," as in a sort of misshapen villanelle, finally uttering the phrase "down to the sea" as if it had been previously repressed.

The second, rear room into which we are allowed a glimpse is furnished—almost crowded—with solid detail. It takes up less canvas in the painting, but more poetic space in the text, delivering its own monologue, brooding over its relation to the silent but more open front room, acknowledging, questioning, exploring, but coming down at the end to the inescapability of the sea, the sky, and the inexorable horizon they meet to create. JH

Serial

Stephen Sandy

At one end altogether of whatever
length the strip could possibly be

you might follow the song of the warbler
like a thread paid out

like a line beautifully cast on a calm sea
specular in fiery noon

following in toward source, quarry,
judgment seat.

*

A line of birds had been drawn
over the horizon. Who could tell

where it had gone? The boy on the sailfish
was a dot on the past. You may not know

where it was he stood.
The length of a thread; the where you are.

Mark Rothko's paintings are saturated with meaning. Both atmospheric and colorful, they denote states of mind, but also echo place and times of our memories. This particular painting is drenched with the colors of a sunset, the end of the day. Memories of ephemeral moments are captured here eternally and we bask in perpetual enjoyment of these fleeting passages. As an object this painting contains the possibilities of retaining beauty and becomes a container that refuses to let the day obey its natural order, so that we might still redeem what has not yet been completed. JW

Poems that speak to or for abstract art have been rare in the past, and it is only the most recent generations of writers who have attempted readings of them. Of the several poems in this volume which confront abstract art of various sorts, Stephen Sandy's poem is itself perhaps the most "abstract" of these, in its acutely nondiscursive response to Rothko's painting. It certainly does not attempt to construe the forms iconographically—windows or façades, for example—nor even consider the relative proportions of the fields of color, or the ghost of the upper rectangle inhabiting the lower square. But rather, perhaps taking a faint cue from an obvious way of characterizing one of Rothko's narrower horizontals as a "strip," the poem takes it and as it were runs with it, spinning it out associatively. A strip, a thread, a line, it connects a series of images, musical, piscatorial, stretching clew-like through a national labyrinth, or, finally, constituting the very frail connectedness of both childhood memories and an ongoing sense of "the where you are." In form, the poem is really a kind of minimal sonnet: fourteen short free-verse lines in discrete couplets, grouped into a clear octave-sestet division. Whether the typographic format that results—a longer stanza followed by a shorter one—mirrors inversely is dubious, but irrelevant. It is rather the unpeeling of the strip or stripe into a line of poetic thought that marks this poem's unique relation to a painted object. JH

Islands Number Four

Elizabeth Alexander

1.

Agnes Martin, *Islands Number Four,*
Repeated ovals on a grid, what appears
To be perfect is handmade, disturbed.
Tobacco brown saturates canvas to burlap,
Clean form from a distance, up close, her hand.
All wrack and bramble to oval and grid.
Hollows in the body, containers for grief.
What looks to be perfect is not perfect.

Odd oval portholes that flood with light.

2.

Description of a Slave Ship. 1789:
Same imperfect ovals, calligraphic hand.
At a distance, pattern. Up close, bodies
Doubled and doubled, serried and stacked
In the manner of galleries in a church.
In full ships on their sides or on each other.
Isle of woe, two-by-two, spoon-fashion,
Not unfrequently found dead in the morning.
Slave-ships, the not-pure, imperfect ovals,
Portholes through which they would never see home.
The flesh rubbed off their shoulders, elbows, hips.
Barracoon, sarcophagus, indestructible grief
Nesting in the hollows of the abdomen.
The slave-ship empty, its cargo landed
And sold for twelve ounces of gold a-piece

Or gone overboard. Islands. Aftermath.

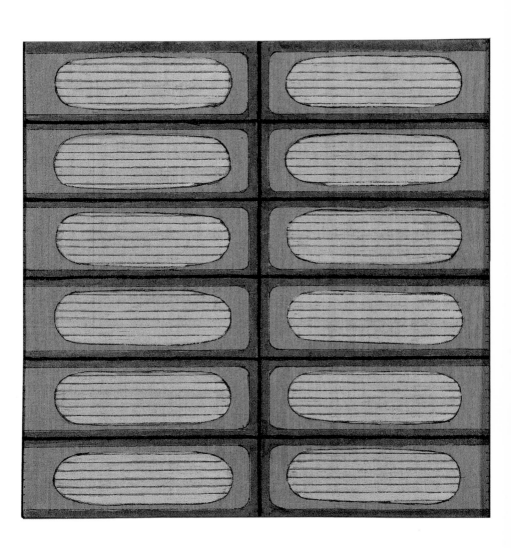

Agnes Martin
(American, born Canada, 1912)

Islands No. 4, ca. 1961
Oil on canvas
37.8 x 37.8 cm
Gift of the Woodward Foundation
1977.49.16

Although Agnes Martin is often called a Minimalist, she sees herself as an Abstract Expressionist. Martin says her paintings are about "freedom from the cares of this world, meant to help people," before daily care strikes. The horizontal line she uses so frequently is the horizon of the prairie, the ocean, or the plain. In this painting, the repetition of this line within the simple geometric form of oval capsules encased in a grid shows an archipelago of islands organized as neatly as if they were in an ice cube tray. But isolation is not alienation. The small scale of this work, in her signature square formation, visually reads as an abbreviated larger work whose tightness defies the limitations of actual canvas size and extends beyond the borders of the frame. JW

One of the immediate questions posed by Agnes Martin's abstract forms—not so much "ovals" as rectangular forms with ends rounded off in arcs—is the basic one of figure/ground, whether their light tone is showing through vertically barred openings in a dark plane or, rather, generated by strips of light substance overlaid upon it. What the poem here chooses to notice is that the forms are, on even the slightest closer inspection, far from being identical, and that it is only six strips that they share in common. The first strophe comes down to a reading of the forms as strangely elongated barred portholes, but allowing for the crucial changes in appearance: "Clean form from a distance, up close, her [the artist's] hand." It characterizes the forms as "Hollows in the body, containers for grief" and as "Odd oval portholes that flood with light."

But the poem then moves to take a second look not so much *at* as *through* the first stanza and its "body," "grief," "portholes," and the title "Islands" (the painter's own half-iconic way of construing the "ovals" in the painting): these lead to a remembered or even imagined text that brings these free-floating images together in a dreadful context—the "Islands," for example, can be literally Caribbean ones or, figuratively, the ships, perhaps even the uprooted persons of the slaves themselves (a "barracoon" is a slave-barracks). But it is in the final "Aftermath" of the sea voyage, the landing and the holding pen, that the major horror begins.
JH

FRANZ KLINE: Ravenna

Stephen Burt

Not a hillside but a hill: depth and a bridge
aslant and flexible, propped up on a ledge
from which the night comes on too soon to judge.
Our world has one side and one edge.
Against it, our rectangular dwellings emerge.

*

Motherly black against taut malachite,
coarse eggshell over smooth egg-white:

snowmelt salutes the recent citizens
and saturates the fogbound sky.

What ice remains recedes in parallel lines.

The gap between Ninth Avenue and the Bronx
is the leap of a lynx
across a valley in the Appenines.

*

Much water with no visible source
falls from one side
of an elevated subway trestle's shade; its flow or force
comes generously, heedlessly, then plaits,
splits, and collides

with the ground-down, washed-out, excavated grates
of 207th Street. Its two bent streams
entwine to shape a third: a shaft or beam
in its own eye. A birthright, or hard work.
The tine inside a ringing tuning fork.

Kline often named his paintings after towns and cities. Inspired by his trip
to Italy in 1960, where his one-man exhibition at the XXX Biennale in
Venice represented the United States, he named several of his paintings
after Italian cities. *Ravenna* incorporates Kline's signature use of shades
of black and white with its quick, deep strokes, to which he added green.
Here the horizontal black paint dominates as a sculptural form and the
almost perpendicular vertical divides this painting into several planes.
Likewise, the brushwork accentuates the action of the painter in executing
this work. The green he used is the same green found in the mosaics of
the fifth- and sixth-century churches and baptisteries in Ravenna. JW

Kline's black-on-white (and often white-on-black-on-white) paintings present invitations to read their blacknesses as calligraphic signs and then withdraw those invitations in the same instant of gesture toward the viewer's eye. Stephen Burt's poem does not presume simplistically to construe the black marks on the white surface as signs; rather, it contemplates the whole field of view, seeing it as a remembered, significant prospect of his own. The location in question is a winter view from an elevated stop on a subway line at the very north of Manhattan looking northeast toward the Bronx. (It has nothing to do, anecdotally or biographically, with the life of Franz Kline.) In describing the scene he is observing, the poet occasionally seems to be giving an expressive reading of Kline's painting (particularly at "Motherly black against taut malachite, / coarse eggshell over smooth egg-white") but then returns to its specific location again. (Burt's poem is in rhymed iambic pentameter with a few variations: one longer, five shorter lines; the well-placed imperfect or off-rhymes—side/collides, plaits/gates, streams/beam; the couplet just quoted stands out from the rest.) The reader keeps feeling that the New York scene is being seen through the painting, as well as vice versa. JH

A Short History of Sex on Campus

for Phil West

Craig Arnold

We had ideas and excuses, axes
and millstones to grind them on
around our necks. We wouldn't think
to wake up in the morning without a cause
to soap our faces with. We talked hard,
we talked fast, we steeled ourselves
to distance, fencers, always on our guard,
we made a habit of breaking habits,
teaching ourselves to tell apart earth-tones
—slate from taupe, beige from sand—
we keyed and calibrated our expectation
to color turned down and volume muted.

The things that puzzled, made our eyes
cloudy, our jaws hang open, faces
unmuscle themselves to putty,
as if to let flow past our senses
what we weren't able to absorb:
The bad joke with a cut of truth.
The tearful ending. The lost temper.
The sculpture of a lipstick on a tank
shameless, erect, so textbook phallic,
the cock we didn't want to have
at either end of having. Whatever it was
we were against it, tanks and the men who shot them,
lipstick in any flavor. How it drew us,
dared us to make light of its silly myth
—hardly a weekend morning wouldn't find it
festooned and garlanded with lingerie,
sprayed with shaving cream, toilet paper
hung in streamers to copy the spurt.

Hardly morning, that time you broke
to giggles below her window, to the cling of pipe
struck by a rubber sole, to the roommate
twisting her sheets against the far wall,
tired of faking sleep—and caught
naked, beside yourself, you slipped

out of the tangle of her sopped-dark hair,
the lips pinked furious as if with blush,
trickling out the first clots of jissom
you'd ever loosened in anyone.

All of a sudden you had to own your body.

A body you dressed and walked out
into the world, yesterday's socks
clamming up to its feet, its knuckles
swollen from stopped-up sleep, to face
what blocked your way, the lipstick,
newly ridiculous: over the orange head
twisted up from the sheath, someone had slipped
a condom of plastic garbage bags.
Something had slapped you. How your face
screwed up can't be described, except as past
embarrassment, a comic mask
to cover the seamy stitching of the body's
qualms and shudders, a butterfly
pasted over the caterpillar nub
of blunt flesh. And yet, and yet

under the bitter and the sweets that coat it,
under the sour renunciations,
far back in a corner of the mouth
the tongue tip can't quite reach, you felt
the well of something unsuspected,
known or unknown as your own blood,
a taste electric as the licked
prongs of a battery—and the taste
was salty, yes, and yes, the taste
was joy.

Claes Thure Oldenburg
(American, born Sweden, 1929)

Lipstick (Ascending) on Caterpillar Tracks, 1969
Reworked 1974
Painted steel body, aluminum tube and fiberglass tip
Gift of the Colossal Keepsake Corporation
1974.86

Lipstick plays with sexuality and monumentalizes a stick of lipstick, mixing gender-coded objects and making a satirical commentary on war in general, and the Vietnam war in particular, epitomizing a generation's reaction to the establishment. This sculpture was intended as a hoax. Originally, the lipstick could be inflated and rendered firm. In this second version, he transforms the creamy quality of lipstick into a hard-edged metal shaft. JW

Claes Oldenburg's joyfully ecstatic pieces of comic sculpture depend for their effect upon two major alterations in their somewhat generalized representations of ordinary objects, namely, changes in material and in scale. His giant lipstick, open and ready to be applied, is "tank"-like in two ways: a tall cylindrical container with handholds for maintenance, mounted on the caterpillar treads of a military vehicle. It was positioned outside administration buildings at Yale in 1970, a time of ferment, by protesting students. Probably ignorant of Oldenburg's oeuvre generally, and thinking of him mindlessly as a "pop artist," they gave the piece a reductive reading as merely punning visually on an erect penis, and counted on the offense they knew it would give certain Yale administrators to effect some kind of punishment.

Craig Arnold's poem unfolds a moment of encounter with Oldenburg's object, set in a later time (the late 1980s) with a later temper ("teaching ourselves to tell apart earth-tones . . . we keyed and calibrated our expectations / to the color turned down and the volume muted"). Leaving the scene of love-making, the protagonist finds that an obvious, unimaginative but inevitable prank has been played on the lipstick, an addition that neither truly desecrates the piece nor really fulfills its promises. But the effect on him is far different from any old story of embarrassment or disillusion, even as it implicitly confirms the more general exuberance of the work of art itself. JH

Opposite Corners

after Sylvia Plimack Mangold

Rika Lesser

I. *Edginess*

In the one opposite,
if mirrors can be believed,
we've passed or gone through (*bro-
ken*'s too jagged a word) the look-in-
glass and are in that room
behind the mirror
                          Or else the room zig-
zags   Or else a squared pillar—of Flame *at the
White Heat?*—congeals in the opposite corner

      The room is empty
      thus you are not there
      but should be

      A third eye hovers
      well above the frame
      reckoning with
      perspectives   *(Which
      calipers?   Whose rules?)*

Reason's not reason enough
that the painting—and it is a painting,
very much a painting about painting—
appeals to me, poet, maker, shaper
that I am

II. *Disappearance*

Is this how we look inside: empty and
unimaginable, and clean?
Full of reflective—self-reflexive?—tricks
vistas that open but do not exist?
My portrait!
Cover the mirror, there has been a death
Unveil the mirror   *Just let go the Breath*
into the glass   Your absence—conspicuous
Empty everything out impulsively

Empty everything out but carefully
Can one be too careful—too serious?
Both possible and real: this Emptiness
Time to clear out
Words grow too heavy for us

III. *Sight Unseen*

I view your canvas after my father's death:
How different in the flesh! Closer to square!
A pale gray shadow broods over the mirror
on a white abyss cropped from the photograph
The floor a sea of planks, pine more gold than red,
on which a lustrous trapezoid floats, listing
to the left   Above the baseboard the paint dips,
the mark of masking tape? In the glass one board
collects a burnished drip of acrylic paint
I think I see a ghost, an afterimage,
a mote in the eye, a gleam—a bare hint of
the opposite corner in the floor's high sheen
        You created this work
        three years earlier than
        a seminal drawing
        in your own collection:
        With a Vanishing Point
        of 66",
        where two metal rulers,
        both so-called *EXACT*, pro-
        pagate others—a field
        of more abstract measures,
        inscribed for your father,
        "diminished at 66"

Call this *Mourning and Marginalia*
Call it *Crossing the Styx:*
        Emptiness clear, a gas
        expanding   Emptiness
        ordered, composition
        extending   Into what
        we don't know, cannot
        ever know   Now turn
        the page, go on   *Release*
        the soul

Sylvia Plimack Mangold
(American, born 1938)

Opposite Corners, 1973
Acrylic on canvas
198.1 x 141.9 cm
Susan Morse Hilles Fund
1974.18

Mangold's mirror sculpturally molds the surrounding physical space. Standing in front of the painting, we expect to see ourselves. The absence of our own reflection causes us to pause and consider in greater detail the painterly quality of the surface. The simplicity of the composition keeps our attention on the exquisitely painted wood floor, uncluttering our own mental space and grounding us on this solid floor. JW

A poet's extrinsic knowledge—about the oeuvre of the artist in question, about the history of art generally—can enter an ecphrastic poem in various ways even about the provenance of the painting in question (a poem of Herman Melville's on a landscape painting by W. S. Gifford that had been owned by John Wilkes Booth's brother Edwin, the actor, led Melville to read the storm scene in retrospect as the approaching Civil War). In this case, Rika Lesser's acquaintance with a later but related work by Sylvia Mangold leads her to the third section of her poem. The first parts have previously moved from the immediate agenda of the edges presented in the painting (of floorboards and walls and their reflections in the perspectivally paradoxical world of the tilted mirror, the hedging of the mirror frame itself, etc.), through the disappearances generated by perspective, or trompe-l'oeil, of a third spatial dimension "in" mirrors and paintings alike. But then "disappearance" becomes a mortal matter: the association of the later drawing and the earlier work leads to the matter of the death—the "disappearance"—of the poet's own father.

    The poem comes to associate painting's degree of visual trickery with its own lexical contrivances, the wordplay earlier in the poem (the punning "edginess" of the section title; the enjambed "*bro-* / *ken*" and "look-in- /glass"; the subsequent movement into tight and near rhyme—even the ironic allusion to Freud's essay "Mourning and Melancolia" near the end), and the second part closes proleptically with "Words grow too heavy for us." JH

Contributors

Jonathan Aaron (PH.D. from Yale 1974) is associate professor of writing, literature, and publishing at Emerson College. A past recipient of grants from the National Endowment for the Arts and the Massachusetts Arts Council, he is the author of two books of poems, *Second Sight* (1982) and *Corridor* (1992), and he is completing a new collection. His recent work has been included in *Best Poems for 1998* and *The Best of the Best American Poetry, 1988–1997*.

Elizabeth Alexander graduated from Yale College in 1984. She is the author of three books of poems, *The Venus Hottentot* (1990), *Body of Life* (1996), and *Antebellum Dream Book* (2001). She has published many essays on African American literature and culture. She is presently visiting lecturer in the African American Studies Department at Yale.

Craig Arnold graduated from Yale College in 1990. His first collection of poems, *Shells*, was the 1998 volume of the Yale Series of Younger Poets. He has been awarded the Amy Lowell Poetry Traveling Scholarship, as well as fellowships from the National Endowment for the Arts, Bread Loaf, and the Texas Institute of Letters. He is currently a Hodder Fellow in the Humanities at Princeton.

George Bradley graduated from Yale College in 1975 and subsequently attended the University of Virginia on the Balch Fellowship for writing. He has published three volumes of verse: *Terms to Be Met* (1986), *Of the Knowledge of Good and Evil* (1991), and *The Fire Fetched Down* (1996). In addition, Bradley is the editor of *The Yale Younger Poets Anthology* (1998). A fourth book of his verse, *Some Assembly Required*, is forthcoming from Knopf in 2001. Among the awards Bradley has received are: the Yale Younger Poets Prize (1985), the Witter Bynner Prize from the American Academy and Institute of Arts and Letters, the Peter I. B. Lavan award from the Academy of American Poets, an Ingram Merrill Prize, and a grant from the National Endowment for the Humanities. Bradley lives with his wife and child in Chester, Connecticut.

John Burt was born in Washington, D.C., in 1955 and raised in Hartford. He received a B.S. from Yale College in biochemistry in 1977 and a PH.D. in English in 1983. Currently he is professor of English at Brandeis University. He is the editor of *The Collected Poems of Robert Penn Warren*, and the author of two books of poems, *The Way Down* (1988) and *Work without Hope* (1996). His current projects are an analysis of the Lincoln-Douglas debates (Lincoln, Douglas, and the Political Culture of Freedom), and a new volume of verse, *The Melian Dialogue*.

Stephen Burt received his PH.D. in English from Yale in 2000; he is now assistant professor of English at Macalester College in St. Paul, Minnesota. His book of poems is *Popular Music* (1999). He is currently writing a book about Randall Jarrell.

Stephen Cushman received his PH.D. in English from Yale in 1982 and is now professor of English at the University of Virginia. He is the author of two volumes of poetry, *Blue Pajamas* (1998) and *Cussing Lesson* (forthcoming 2002); two volumes of literary criticism, *William Carlos Williams and the Meanings of Measure* (1985) and *Fictions of Form in American Poetry* (1993); and *Bloody Promenade: Reflections on a Civil War Battle* (1999).

Annie Finch received her B.A. from Yale College in 1979, an M.A. from Houston in 1986 and a PH.D. from Stanford in 1990. Currently she is associate professor at Miami University of Ohio. Her books of poetry include *Eve* (1997); the forthcoming epic poem *Marie Moving* (2002); *Calendars* (a 2000 National Poetry Series finalist); and a translation of the complete poems of Renaissance poet Louise Labé. She has also published a critical book on poetics, *The Ghost of Meter*, and edited four anthologies of and about poetry including *A Formal Feeling Comes: Poems in Form by Contemporary Women*, now in its sixth printing, and the forthcoming *An Exaltation of Forms: Contemporary Poets Celebrate the Diversity of Their Art*. Her poems and translations have been published in *The Paris Review*, *Prairie Schooner*, *Poetry*, *Field*, *Agni Review*, *Thirteen Moon*, *The Kenyon Review*, *Partisan Review*, and many other journals and anthologies, and she has collaborated with composers on an opera libretto, a cantata, and several musical settings of poems.

John Hollander was born in New York City in 1929 and educated at Columbia University (A.B. 1950, M.A. 1952) and Indiana University (PH.D., 1959). He was a Junior Fellow of Harvard's Society of Fellows from 1954 to 1957. Currently Sterling Professor of English at Yale, he is the author of eighteen books of poetry, including, most recently, *Figurehead, Tessarae, Selected Poetry*, and a new edition of his *Reflections on Espionage*. The most recent of his nine volumes of criticism are *The Work of Poetry* and *The Poetry of Everyday Life*. He has written extensively about American art and artists (among them Edward Hopper, Saul Steinberg, and William Bailey) and has edited or co-edited twenty-one books, including *American Poetry: The Nineteenth Century* and *The Oxford Anthology of English Literature*. Among his awards are the Bollingen Prize for Poetry and a MacArthur Fellowship.

Martha Hollander graduated from Yale College in 1980. She was awarded many student poetry prizes by Yale and the University of California at Berkeley, where she received a PH.D. in art history in

1990. Her first collection of poems, *The Game of Statues* (1990) received the Walt Whitman Award from the Academy of American Poets. She is also the author of a chapbook, *Always History* (1985). Her poems have appeared in various anthologies and major periodicals. An art historian, Hollander is the author of numerous essays and articles on seventeenth-century Dutch art. Currently she teaches art history and humanities at Hofstra University and lives with her husband and two sons in Jackson Heights, New York.

Paul Kane received his B.A. from Yale College in 1973 and returned in 1986 for graduate work in English (M.A. 1987, M. PHIL. 1988, PH.D. 1990). As an undergraduate he attended classes with fellow poets George Bradley, Rika Lesser, William Logan, and J. D. McClatchy. He has since published seven books, including two collections of poems, *The Farther Shore* and *Drowned Lands*. His other publications include two editions of Emerson's works with the Library of America; an anthology, *Poetry of the American Renaissance*; a critical study, *Australian Poetry: Romanticism and Negativity*; and *A Hudson Landscape*, a collaboration with the photographer William Clift. His awards include a Fulbright scholarship to Australia and fellowships from the National Endowment for the Humanities and the Guggenheim Foundation. From 1979 to 1980 he and his wife lived with the artist and designer Ilonka Karasz. A professor of English at Vassar College, he lives in Warwick, New York.

Karl Kirchwey is the author of three books of poems: *A Wandering Island* (1990; recipient of the Poetry Society of America's Norma Farber First Book Award); *Those I Guard* (1993) and *The Engrafted Word* (1998). His work-in-progress based on the *Alcestis* of Euripides received the *Paris Review*'s first Prize for Poetic Drama (1997). His poems have been widely anthologized, and his work has been included in *The Best of the Best American Poetry*, a ten-year retrospective (1998). Among his awards and prizes are a Rome Prize in Literature and a Guggenheim Fellowship and grants from the NEA and Ingram Merrill Foundations. Mr. Kirchwey was educated at Yale College (B.A. 1979) and Columbia University (M.A. 1981). From 1987 to 2000 he was Director of the Unterberg Poetry Center of the 92nd Street Y in New York. He has taught at Yale, Columbia, Smith College, and Wesleyan University, and is now Director of Creative Writing and Senior Lecturer in the Arts at Bryn Mawr College.

Rika Lesser was born in Brooklyn, New York, in 1953. She was a Scholar of the House and graduated from Yale College in 1974; she received an M.F.A. in Writing from Columbia University and is a poet and translator of Swedish and German literature. She is the author of three collections of poetry, *Etruscan Things* (1983), *All We Need of Hell* (1995), and *Growing Back: Poems 1972-1992* (1997). Among her translations are works by Ekelöf, Rilke, Hesse, and Sonnev.

Lesser is the recipient of many grants and awards originating here or in Scandinavia—among them the Amy Lowell Poetry Traveling Scholarship, a poetry grant from the Ingram Merrill Foundation, various stipends or prizes from Swedish and Finnish organizations. In 1999 she received a Fulbright Fellowship to Sweden, and in 2001 a National Endowment for the Arts Literature Fellowship for Poetry Translation. She lives in Brooklyn Heights but often travels to Sweden, where she continues to consult with Goran Sonnevi on the translation of his *Mozart's Third Brain.*

William Logan received his B.A. from Yale College in 1972 and his M.F.A. from the University of Iowa in 1975. He is the author of five books of poetry, *Sad-faced Men* (1982), *Difficulty* (1985), *Sullen Weedy Lakes* (1988), *Vain Empires* (1998), and *Night Battle* (1999), as well as two books of essays and reviews, *All the Rage* (1998) and *Reputations of the Tongue* (1999), the latter a finalist for the National Book Critics Circle award in criticism. He received the Peter I. B. Lavan Younger Poets Award from the Academy of American Poets, and the Citation for Excellence in Reviewing from the National Book Critics Circle. He has written an introduction to an expanded edition of Randall Jarrell's *Poetry and the Age*, which will appear in 2001. He teaches at the University of Florida, where he is Alumni/ae Professor of English.

J. D. McClatchy received his PH.D from Yale in 1974. He is the author of four collections of poems: *Scenes From Another Life* (1981), *Stars Principal* (1986), *The Rest of the Way* (1990), and *Ten Commandments* (1998). His literary essays are collected in *White Paper* (1989), which earned him the Melville Cane Award by the Poetry Society of America, and in *Twenty Questions* (1998). He has edited many books, and since 1991, he has served as editor of *The Yale Review.* In 1996 he was named a Chancellor of the Academy of American Poets, and in 1998 he was elected a Fellow of the American Academy of Arts and Sciences. The following year he was elected to membership in the American Academy of Arts and Letters. Mr. McClatchy, who lives in Stonington, Connecticut, has been awarded the Arts Medal by the State of Connecticut.

Peter Sacks received his PH.D. from Yale in 1980. He is the author of four collections of poems, most recently *O Wheel* (2000) and *Natal Command* (1997), as well as *The English Elegy: Studies in the Genre from Spenser to Yeats*, and a number of essays on poetry, and on painting. Born in South Africa, he taught at The Johns Hopkins University, and currently he is a professor in the Department of English and American Literature and Language at Harvard.

Tony Sanders was born in New York City. A member of Yale's class of 1979, his poems and reviews have appeared in a wide number of periodicals, including *The Yale Review, Harvard Review, Poetry, Gettysburg*

Review, Grand Street, The New Republic, and *Chelsea.* "The Warning Track," which won the Bernard F. Conners prize for the long poem, appeared in *The Paris Review.* His first collection, *Partial Eclipse* (1994), won the Vassar Miller Prize. His second collection, *Transit Authority,* was published in spring 2000.

Stephen Sandy's collections of poems include *Stresses in the Peaceable Kingdom* (1967); *Roofs* (1971), *End of the Picaro* (1977), *Riding to Greylock* (1983), *Man in the Open Air* (1988), *Thanksgiving over the Water* (1992), *The Thread, New and Selected Poems* (1998), *Black Box* (1999), and *Race Point* (forthcoming 2002). Sandy is the author of *The Raveling of the Novel, Studies in Romantic Fiction* (1980) and *A Cloak for Hercules,* a verse translation of Seneca's *Hercules Oetaeus* (1995). He collaborated with the composer Henry Brant on *Vita De Sancta Hieronymo, An Antiphonal Cantata* (1973). Sandy has been awarded an NEA Fellowship, an Ingram Merrill Foundation Fellowship, a Fulbright Lecturership, a Dexter Fellowship, Vermont Council on the Arts Fellowships, and an Academy of American Poets College Prize. He was Phi Beta Kappa Poet at Brown University. Sandy holds degrees from Yale University (B.A. 1955) and Harvard University (A.M. 1959, PH.D. 1963). He served in the Army, and he has been on the faculties of Harvard University, Brown University, University of Tokyo, University of Rhode Island, Davidson College, and Bennington College.

Robert B. Shaw was a graduate student of English at Yale (M.PHIL. 1973, PH.D. 1974). After two years of teaching at Harvard, where he earned his B.A., he returned to Yale to teach in the English department from 1976 to 1983. Among his students at Yale were the poets John Burt and Tony Sanders. In 1983 Shaw joined the English department at Mount Holyoke College, where he now is a professor of English. His books of poems are *Comforting the Wilderness* (1977), *The Wonder of Seeing Double* (1988), *The Post Office Murals Restored* (1994), and *Below the Surface* (1999). He also has published a critical study of Donne and Herbert and numerous articles and reviews, mostly on twentieth-century poetry. His awards include fellowships from the National Endowment for the Arts and the Ingram Merrill Foundation, and the James Boatwright III Prize for poetry.

David R. Slavitt is a member of the Yale College class of 1956, and was a Scholar of the House. He has an M.A. from Columbia University, and currently he is a member of the faculty of Bennington College in Vermont. His numerous publications include, most recently, *Falling from Silence* (2001), *The Book of Lamentations* (2001), and *The Sonnets of Love and Death of Jean de Sponed* (2001).

Rosanna Warren is the Emma MacLachlan Metcalf Professor of the Humanities at Boston University. Her most recent publications are

Suppliant Women, by Euripides (translated with Stephen Scully), and *Stained Glass*, poems. She is a Chancellor of the Academy of American Poets. In 2000–2001, she is Resident in Literature and Visiting Scholar at the American Academy in Rome.

Joanna Weber is the Assistant Curator of European and Contemporary Art at the Yale University Art Gallery. She received a Masters of Religion and the Visual Arts from Yale Divinity School in 1989. In 2000 she was the organizing curator for the exhibition *Philip Guston: A New Alphabet, the Late Transition*. She recently received a grant from the Lannan Foundation to write a book on *Making Space for the Sacred: The Agnes Martin Gallery at the Harwood Museum in Taos, New Mexico*.

Rachel Wetzsteon received a B.A. from Yale in 1989, an M.A. from the Johns Hopkins Writing Seminars in 1990, and a PH.D. from Columbia in 1999. Her first book of poems, *The Other Stars*, won the 1993 National Poetry Series and was published in 1994; her second book, *Home and Away*, was published in 1998. She has received an Ingram Merrill grant, and her poems have appeared in such publications as *The New Republic*, *The New Yorker*, *The Paris Review*, and *The Yale Review*. She is an assistant professor of English at Iona College in New Rochelle, and lives in New York City.

Works of art by artist

Pierre Bonnard, *Interior at Le Cannet*, 1938.

Alexander Calder, *Cat*, ca. 1930.

Salvador Dalí, *The Phantom Cart*, 1933.

Marcel Duchamp, *In advance of the broken arm (Snow Shovel)*, 1945.

Walker Evans, *Lexington Avenue Subway*, 1941.

Alberto Giacometti, *Hands Holding the Void*, 1934.

Edward Hopper, *Rooms by the Sea*, 1951.

Ilonka Karasz, *Tea and Coffee Service*, ca. 1928.

Franz Kline, *Ravenna*, 1961.

Georg Kolbe, *Kneeling Woman (Kniende)*, 1926.

Käthe Kollwitz, *The Ploughmen*, 1906.

Kasimir Malevich, *The Knifegrinder*, 1912–13.

Sylvia Plimack Mangold, *Opposite Corners*, 1973.

Agnes Martin, *Islands No. 4*, ca. 1961.

Claes Thure Oldenburg, *Lipstick (Ascending) on Caterpillar Tracks*, 1969, reworked 1974.

Jackson Pollock, *Number 13A: Arabesque*, 1948.

Mark Rothko, *Untitled*, 1954.

Kurt Schwitters, *Merzz. 19*, 1920.

Joseph Stella, *Spring (The Procession)*, ca. 1914–16.

Sophie Taeuber-Arp, *Turned Wood Sculpture*, 1937.

Unknown artist, *Lutumbo Iwa Kindi Image*, 20th century.

Edward Weston, *Squash*, 1936.

This book is set in Postscript Monotype Bulmer. Bulmer was originally cut as a foundry type by William Martin about 1790 for William Bulmer of the Shakespeare Press. Monotype issued a revival for the Monotype machine designed by Morris Benton, and the Postscript revival is a variant of this font.